Japan Travel Guide

BnW Travel Series

Ashok Kumawat

Disclaimer:

The information provided in this Japan travel guide is based on extensive research and the author's personal experiences. However, travel conditions, prices, and availability of attractions, accommodations, and services may change over time. While every effort has been made to ensure the accuracy and reliability of the information, the author and publisher cannot be held responsible for any inaccuracies or changes that may occur after the publication of this guide. It is recommended to double-check with official sources and make your own informed decisions when planning your trip. The author and publisher are not liable for any losses, injuries, or damages incurred as a result of using the information provided in this guide. Travelers are encouraged to exercise caution, follow local laws and customs, and obtain appropriate travel insurance before embarking on their journey to Japan.

Table of contents:

Introduction to Japan: Land of Tradition and Innovation

Japan, a captivating archipelago nestled in the heart of the Pacific Ocean, is a land of rich traditions, awe-inspiring landscapes, and cutting-edge technology. From the moment you set foot in this captivating country, you will be immersed in a unique blend of ancient customs and modern advancements, creating an enchanting experience like no other.

Geographically, Japan consists of four main islands, Honshu, Hokkaido, Kyushu, and Shikoku, along with thousands of smaller islands. Each region has its own distinct charm and attractions, offering a diverse range of experiences to the discerning traveler.

Steeped in a history spanning thousands of years, Japan proudly preserves its cultural heritage. Traditional arts, such as tea ceremonies, calligraphy, and ikebana (flower arranging), continue to thrive, showcasing the meticulous craftsmanship and attention to detail that define Japanese aesthetics.

One of the most remarkable aspects of Japanese culture is its unwavering commitment to respect and etiquette. Politeness and mindfulness permeate every aspect of daily life, from bowing when greeting someone to meticulously following social customs. Learning a few basic phrases in Japanese, such as "Konnichiwa" (hello) and "Arigatou gozaimasu" (thank you very much), will go a long way in fostering positive interactions and showing appreciation for the local culture.

The juxtaposition of tradition and innovation is perhaps most evident in Japan's bustling metropolises. Tokyo, the capital city, pulsates with an energy that is both invigorating and captivating. Skyscrapers reach for the sky, futuristic neon signs illuminate the streets, and bustling marketplaces offer a sensory overload of sights, sounds, and flavors. Yet amidst the modernity, ancient shrines and temples stand as tranquil reminders of Japan's spiritual roots.

Kyoto, the former imperial capital, offers a glimpse into Japan's glorious past. With its UNESCO World Heritage sites, including the iconic Kinkaku-ji Temple (Golden Pavilion) and the serene Arashiyama Bamboo Grove, Kyoto transports visitors to a bygone era of samurais and geishas. Exploring the city's traditional neighborhoods, such as Gion, allows you to witness the artistry and grace of geisha culture, with the possibility of catching a glimpse of these elusive entertainers.

Beyond the cities, Japan's natural beauty is equally captivating. The country boasts majestic mountains, picturesque countryside, and pristine coastlines. The iconic Mount Fuji, an emblem of Japan's identity, invites adventurers to conquer its heights or simply appreciate its splendor from afar. In contrast, the northern region of Hokkaido showcases a different side of Japan, with its rugged wilderness, hot springs, and abundant wildlife. Exploring Hokkaido's national parks, such as Shiretoko and Daisetsuzan, offers a chance to connect with nature in its purest form.

Japanese cuisine is renowned worldwide for its exquisite flavors and artful presentation. Sushi, sashimi, ramen, and tempura are just a few of the delectable dishes that await food enthusiasts. Each region boasts its own culinary specialties, providing a diverse gastronomic journey. From the vibrant seafood markets of Tsukiji in Tokyo to the street food stalls of Osaka's Dotonbori district, Japan's culinary scene is a sensory delight that should not be missed.

Japan's transportation infrastructure is renowned for its efficiency and reliability, making it easy to explore the country. The extensive network of bullet trains, known as shinkansen, connects major cities with remarkable speed, allowing travelers to traverse the country with ease. Additionally, local trains, buses, and subways provide convenient access to even the most remote regions.

Safety is a top priority in Japan, and visitors can feel secure knowing that crime rates are low and public spaces are well-maintained. The country's healthcare system is also world-class, ensuring that travelers receive the necessary care if needed.

In this comprehensive Japan travel guide, we will delve deeper into the enchanting facets of this remarkable country. From the vibrant streets of Tokyo to the serene temples of Kyoto, from the snow-capped peaks of the Japanese Alps to the tranquil beauty of its gardens, each chapter will provide insights, practical tips, and recommendations to help you make the most of your journey through Japan.

So, prepare yourself for an extraordinary adventure as we embark on a captivating exploration of Japan's traditions, innovations, and the unparalleled experiences that await you in this land of ancient charm and modern marvels.

Planning Your Trip to Japan: Tips and Essentials

Embarking on a journey to Japan is an exciting endeavor filled with endless possibilities. As you prepare for your trip to this captivating country, proper planning and essential knowledge will ensure a smooth and memorable experience. In this chapter, we will provide you with invaluable tips and essential information to help you make the most of your adventure in Japan.

Visa Requirements:

Before traveling to Japan, it is crucial to determine the visa requirements based on your nationality. Citizens of many countries are eligible for visa-free travel to Japan for a limited period. However, some nationalities may require a tourist visa in advance. Make sure to check the official website of the Japanese embassy or consulate in your home country for the most up-to-date information.

Best Time to Visit:

Japan experiences distinct seasons, each offering its own unique charm. Spring (March to May) is renowned for the mesmerizing cherry blossoms, while autumn (September to November) showcases vibrant foliage. Summer (June to August) brings warm weather and lively festivals, while winter (December to February) invites visitors to witness breathtaking snowscapes. Consider your preferences and the activities you wish to engage in when choosing the best time to visit.

Duration of Stay:

Determining the duration of your stay is essential for effective trip planning. Japan offers an abundance of attractions and experiences, and ideally, you should allocate at least a week to explore Tokyo and Kyoto. However, if time permits, extending your visit to two or three weeks will allow for a more comprehensive exploration of the country, including other regions such as Hokkaido, Hiroshima, and Osaka.

Creating an Itinerary:

Japan's diverse regions and cities offer a plethora of experiences. Research and prioritize the destinations and activities that interest you the most, and create an itinerary accordingly. Keep in mind the travel distances and transportation options between cities to ensure a realistic and efficient schedule. Strike a balance between iconic landmarks, cultural immersion, and leisure time to make the most of your journey.

Booking Flights:

When booking flights to Japan, consider both the major international airports in Tokyo (Narita and Haneda) and other regional airports depending on your itinerary. Compare prices from different airlines and look for deals and promotions to secure the best possible fares. It is advisable to book your flights well in advance to guarantee availability, especially during peak travel seasons.

Accommodation Options:

Japan offers a wide range of accommodation options to suit various budgets and preferences. From luxury hotels and traditional ryokans (Japanese inns) to guesthouses and budget-friendly hostels, you will find something to cater to your needs. Consider the location, amenities, and reviews when selecting your accommodations. It is also advisable to book in advance, especially for popular destinations.

Transportation in Japan:

Japan's transportation system is renowned for its efficiency and punctuality. The extensive rail network, including the famous shinkansen (bullet trains), connects major cities and regions. Consider purchasing a Japan Rail Pass (JR Pass) if you plan to travel extensively by train. Local transportation options such as buses and subways are also widely available in urban areas. Familiarize yourself with the transportation routes, schedules, and fare systems to navigate seamlessly throughout the country.

Language and Communication:

While English signage and information are increasingly common in tourist areas, it is still beneficial to learn a few basic Japanese phrases. Polite greetings such as "Konnichiwa" (hello) and "Arigatou gozaimasu" (thank you very much) will be appreciated. Carry a pocket-sized phrasebook or use translation apps to facilitate communication. Additionally, consider renting a portable Wi-Fi device or purchasing a local SIM card for internet access during your stay.

Currency and Money Matters:

The official currency of Japan is the Japanese Yen (JPY). Familiarize yourself with the current exchange rates and be prepared to use cash as credit cards may not be accepted at all establishments, especially smaller shops and restaurants. Conveniently located ATMs are available in cities, and major credit cards are accepted in larger establishments. It is advisable to notify your bank about your travel plans to avoid any issues with card usage.

Safety and Health:

Japan is known for its safety, but it's still important to exercise common sense and take necessary precautions. Familiarize yourself with emergency contact numbers and the locations of nearby hospitals or clinics. It is recommended to have travel insurance that covers medical expenses and trip cancellations. Additionally, check if any specific vaccinations are required before traveling to Japan and carry necessary medications with you.

Cultural Etiquette:

Respecting Japanese customs and etiquette is essential during your visit. Bowing when greeting someone, removing your shoes in certain establishments, and using chopsticks appropriately are some examples of customary practices. It is important to be mindful of noise levels in public spaces and to avoid littering. Familiarize yourself with basic Japanese etiquette to show respect for the local culture.

By considering these essential tips and incorporating them into your trip planning, you will be well-prepared to embark on an unforgettable journey through Japan. The next chapters will delve deeper into the specific regions, attractions, and experiences that await you, ensuring that your adventure in Japan is nothing short of extraordinary.

Japanese Culture and Etiquette: Do's and Don'ts

Japan is a country with a rich cultural heritage and a strong emphasis on respect, politeness, and harmony. Understanding and observing Japanese customs and etiquette will not only enhance your travel experience but also show respect for the local culture. In this chapter, we will explore some essential do's and don'ts to help you navigate Japanese culture with grace and understanding.

Do's:

Bowing: Bowing is an integral part of Japanese culture and a common form of greeting. When meeting someone, it is customary to bow slightly as a sign of respect. The depth of the bow varies depending on the situation and the person's social status. Follow the lead of the Japanese person you are interacting with and return the bow accordingly.

Removing Shoes: In many Japanese homes, traditional restaurants, and certain public spaces such as temples and ryokans, it is customary to remove your shoes before entering. Look for signs indicating whether shoe removal is required, and use the provided slippers or walk in socks or barefoot.

Saying "Arigatou gozaimasu": Expressing gratitude is highly valued in Japanese culture. Use "Arigatou gozaimasu" to say "thank you very much." It is a polite way to show appreciation for services received, gestures made, or favors extended.

Eating Etiquette: When dining in Japan, there are a few important etiquette rules to observe. It is customary to say "Itadakimasu" before starting your meal, which is a way of expressing gratitude for the food. Slurping noodles, particularly ramen, is considered acceptable and even a sign of enjoying the meal. However, avoid loud chewing or talking with a full mouth.

Queuing: Japan is known for its orderly queues, and cutting in line is considered rude. When waiting in line, maintain a respectful distance from the person in front of you and avoid pushing or crowding.

Handling Chopsticks: If you are not accustomed to using chopsticks, it is worth practicing before your trip to Japan. When not in use, rest your chopsticks on the provided chopstick rest or a small plate. Avoid sticking chopsticks vertically into a bowl of rice, as this is reminiscent of funeral rituals.

Observing Silence: In certain public spaces such as trains, buses, and waiting areas, maintaining a quiet and serene atmosphere is appreciated. Use your headphones when listening to music or watching videos, and keep conversations at a low volume to avoid disturbing others.

Don'ts:

Public Displays of Affection: Japan is a culture that values modesty and privacy. Public displays of affection, such as kissing or hugging, are generally not common in public spaces. It is advisable to be mindful of cultural norms and to express affection in a more reserved manner.

Wearing Shoes Inside: As mentioned earlier, removing shoes is customary in many Japanese homes, traditional establishments, and even some modern establishments. Avoid wearing shoes inside unless indicated otherwise. Look for shoe racks or shoe storage areas near entrances.

Pointing with Chopsticks: Pointing at people or objects with chopsticks is considered impolite. If you need to indicate something, use your hand or a verbal cue instead.

Blowing Your Nose in Public: Blowing your nose loudly in public is generally frowned upon in Japan. If you need to blow your nose, it is considered more polite to do so discreetly, such as in a restroom or using a handkerchief or tissue.

Tipping: Unlike in some Western countries, tipping is not customary in Japan. It can be seen as an insult or confusion. Instead, excellent service is expected as a standard, and tipping may even be refused.

Touching People: Japanese people generally maintain a certain personal space. Avoid touching others, especially those you do not have a close relationship with, unless there is a specific cultural context, such as a handshake in a formal setting.

Disrespecting Temples and Shrines: When visiting temples and shrines, show respect by following the designated paths, refraining from touching sacred objects, and maintaining a quiet demeanor. Avoid using flash photography in places where it is prohibited.

By adhering to these do's and don'ts, you will not only navigate Japanese culture smoothly but also demonstrate your respect and appreciation for the customs and traditions of this remarkable country. Embrace the opportunity to immerse yourself in Japanese culture and create lasting memories during your journey.

Best Time to Visit Japan: Weather and Seasonal Highlights

Japan is a country that delights visitors year-round, offering a unique blend of natural beauty and cultural experiences. Each season brings its own distinct charm and showcases different facets of Japan's diverse landscape. In this chapter, we will explore the best times to visit Japan based on weather conditions and highlight the seasonal attractions that await you.

Spring (March to May):

Spring in Japan is synonymous with the blooming of cherry blossoms, known as sakura. This iconic phenomenon attracts visitors from around the world, creating a magical atmosphere. The cherry blossoms typically start blooming in late March in the southern regions of Kyushu and Shikoku, gradually moving northward, reaching Tokyo and Kyoto in early April, and Hokkaido in early May. The cherry blossom season lasts only a short period, usually a week or two, depending on weather conditions. Parks, temples, and riversides become adorned with delicate pink and white petals, offering a picturesque backdrop for hanami (flower-viewing) picnics and strolls. Spring temperatures are mild, ranging from around 10 to 20 degrees Celsius (50 to 68 degrees Fahrenheit), making it an ideal time for exploring cities and enjoying outdoor activities.

Recommended Spring Highlights:

Shinjuku Gyoen National Garden in Tokyo

Philosopher's Path in Kyoto

Hirosaki Castle Park in Aomori Prefecture

Fuji Five Lakes region near Mount Fuji

Summer (June to August):

Summer in Japan brings warm and humid weather, with temperatures ranging from 25 to 35 degrees Celsius (77 to 95 degrees Fahrenheit). It is a season of vibrant festivals, lively fireworks displays, and lush greenery. However, it is important to note that summer also coincides with the rainy season (tsuyu), which lasts from mid-June to mid-July, particularly in the southern and central regions. Despite the occasional rain showers, summer offers a host of exciting experiences. Coastal regions and islands become popular destinations for beach activities and water sports. Mountainous areas offer respite from the heat and provide opportunities for hiking and enjoying picturesque landscapes. The famous Gion Matsuri in Kyoto and the Nebuta Festival in Aomori are just a few of the many colorful festivals that take place during summer.

Recommended Summer Highlights:

Beppu Hot Springs in Oita Prefecture

Amanohashidate in Kyoto Prefecture

Sapporo Beer Garden in Hokkaido

Naoshima Island in the Seto Inland Sea

Autumn (September to November):

Autumn in Japan is a season of breathtaking beauty as the landscapes transform into a vibrant tapestry of red, orange, and gold hues. The cooler temperatures, ranging from 10 to 25 degrees Celsius (50 to 77 degrees Fahrenheit), provide comfortable conditions for outdoor exploration. Autumn foliage, known as koyo, can be observed throughout the country, with the colors starting to change in September in Hokkaido and gradually moving southward, reaching Tokyo and Kyoto in November. Parks, gardens, and mountains become popular spots for nature enthusiasts and photographers seeking to capture the stunning autumn scenery. The autumn season also brings a variety of harvest festivals, celebrating bountiful crops and local traditions.

Recommended Autumn Highlights:

Arashiyama Bamboo Grove in Kyoto

Nikko National Park in Tochigi Prefecture

Daisetsuzan National Park in Hokkaido

Shirakawa-go Village in Gifu Prefecture

Winter (December to February):

Winter in Japan offers a mix of snowy landscapes, festive celebrations, and unique cultural experiences. Northern regions, such as Hokkaido and the Japanese Alps, are known for their heavy snowfall and offer excellent skiing and snowboarding opportunities. The Sapporo Snow Festival in February attracts millions of visitors who come to marvel at the intricate ice sculptures. In cities like Tokyo and Osaka, you can experience the enchanting illuminations and festive decorations during the holiday season. Winter temperatures vary across the country, with average temperatures ranging from 0 to 10 degrees Celsius (32 to 50 degrees Fahrenheit).

Recommended Winter Highlights:

Niseko Ski Resort in Hokkaido

Snow Monkey Park in Nagano Prefecture

Sapporo Winter Sports Museum in Hokkaido

Yokote Kamakura Festival in Akita Prefecture

Regardless of the season you choose to visit, Japan offers a wealth of experiences and attractions that cater to diverse interests. Each season has its own unique charm and provides a different perspective on the beauty and culture of this remarkable country. Consider your preferences, weather conditions, and desired activities when planning your trip to Japan, and get ready to immerse yourself in the wonders that await you.

Discovering Tokyo: A Metropolis of Contrasts

Tokyo, the capital city of Japan, is a vibrant and dynamic metropolis that seamlessly blends tradition and innovation. With its towering skyscrapers, bustling streets, serene gardens, and historical sites, Tokyo offers a diverse range of experiences that captivate the imagination of every traveler. In this chapter, we will delve into the wonders of Tokyo, exploring its iconic landmarks, unique neighborhoods, cultural gems, and culinary delights.

The Imperial Palace and East Gardens:

Start your exploration of Tokyo with a visit to the Imperial Palace and its East Gardens. This historic site, situated in the heart of the city, offers a glimpse into Japan's imperial past. Explore the vast palace grounds, admire the stunning Nijubashi Bridge, and stroll through the meticulously manicured gardens. The East Gardens, with their tranquil ponds, ancient ruins, and seasonal flowers, provide a serene escape from the bustling city.

Shibuya Crossing and Harajuku:

Experience the energy and excitement of Tokyo's famous Shibuya Crossing, often called the busiest intersection in the world. Stand at the center of the chaos and witness the synchronized flow of pedestrians crossing from all directions. Adjacent to Shibuya is Harajuku, a vibrant neighborhood known for its eccentric street fashion, quirky shops, and trendy cafes. Take a leisurely stroll down Takeshita Street, where you'll find a colorful array of boutiques, vintage stores, and crepe stands.

Meiji Shrine and Yoyogi Park:

Just a stone's throw away from Harajuku, you'll find the tranquil oasis of Meiji Shrine and Yoyogi Park. Meiji Shrine, dedicated to Emperor Meiji and Empress Shoken, offers a serene retreat with its towering wooden torii gates and lush forested grounds. Take a leisurely walk through the park, enjoying the peaceful atmosphere and perhaps witnessing a traditional wedding procession. Yoyogi Park, adjacent to the shrine, is a popular spot for picnics, cycling, and people-watching.

Asakusa and Senso-ji Temple:

Step back in time as you visit the historic district of Asakusa. The focal point of this area is Senso-ji, Tokyo's oldest and most revered Buddhist temple. Enter through the magnificent Kaminarimon Gate, adorned with a massive red lantern, and stroll down Nakamise Shopping Street, lined with traditional souvenir shops and food stalls. At the temple, partake in the ritual of cleansing at the chozuya, make a wish at the incense-filled main hall, and soak in the serene atmosphere.

Akihabara and the Electric Town:

For a taste of Tokyo's futuristic side, head to Akihabara, also known as the Electric Town. This district is a paradise for technology enthusiasts and anime fans alike. Explore multistory electronics stores, browse through manga and anime shops, and immerse yourself in the world of gaming at arcades that buzz with excitement. Don't miss the iconic maid cafes, where waitresses dressed in maid costumes provide a unique dining experience.

Tsukiji Fish Market and Ginza:

Indulge in a culinary adventure at the renowned Tsukiji Fish Market, a paradise for seafood lovers. Witness the lively tuna auctions in the early morning and savor the freshest sushi at one of the many sushi restaurants in the area. Afterward, make your way to Ginza, Tokyo's upscale shopping district, where luxury boutiques, department stores, and gourmet restaurants line the streets. Enjoy a shopping spree, visit art galleries, or savor exquisite cuisine at Michelin-starred restaurants.

Shinjuku and Tokyo Metropolitan Government Building:

Experience the vibrant atmosphere of Shinjuku, Tokyo's bustling entertainment and business district. Explore the neon-lit streets, visit Kabukicho, Tokyo's famous red-light district (exercise caution and be mindful of personal safety), and immerse yourself in the energetic ambiance. For a panoramic view of the city, head to the Tokyo Metropolitan Government Building's observation decks, offering breathtaking vistas of the cityscape.

Tokyo's myriad of attractions and neighborhoods offers a wealth of experiences for every traveler. From ancient temples and serene gardens to futuristic technology and bustling streets, this metropolis of contrasts never fails to impress. Immerse yourself in the rich tapestry of Tokyo, and you'll discover a city that embodies the essence of Japan's past, present, and future.

Exploring Kyoto: Ancient Temples and Tranquil Gardens

Kyoto, a city steeped in history and traditional Japanese culture, is a must-visit destination for travelers seeking to immerse themselves in the beauty and serenity of ancient Japan. With its abundance of UNESCO World Heritage sites, majestic temples, and meticulously manicured gardens, Kyoto offers a glimpse into the country's rich cultural heritage. In this chapter, we will embark on a journey to explore the timeless beauty of Kyoto, where ancient traditions harmonize with modern life.

Kinkaku-ji (Golden Pavilion):

Begin your Kyoto adventure with a visit to Kinkaku-ji, also known as the Golden Pavilion. This iconic Zen Buddhist temple is a dazzling sight to behold, with its top two floors covered in brilliant gold leaf. Surrounded by a tranquil pond and a meticulously landscaped garden, Kinkaku-ji exudes an otherworldly beauty that captivates visitors. Take a leisurely stroll around the temple grounds, enjoy the reflections on the water, and immerse yourself in the serenity of this architectural masterpiece.

Fushimi Inari Taisha:

Venture to Fushimi Inari Taisha, one of Kyoto's most important Shinto shrines. Known for its famous torii gate pathway, this sprawling shrine complex is dedicated to Inari, the Shinto god of rice and prosperity. As you ascend the mountain, you'll be greeted by thousands of vibrant red torii gates, creating a mesmerizing tunnel-like path. Explore the various sub-shrines, witness the rituals of worship, and enjoy panoramic views of Kyoto from the mountaintop.

Arashiyama Bamboo Grove:

Find tranquility amidst the towering bamboo stalks of the Arashiyama Bamboo Grove. This enchanting natural wonder is a popular attraction in Kyoto, offering a serene respite from the bustling city. As you walk through the bamboo forest, you'll be greeted by the soothing rustle of leaves, creating a magical atmosphere. Take a leisurely stroll along the pathways, visit nearby temples, and explore the picturesque Arashiyama district.

Kiyomizu-dera Temple:

A visit to Kyoto would be incomplete without experiencing the beauty of Kiyomizu-dera, a UNESCO World Heritage site. Perched on a hillside, this wooden temple offers panoramic views of Kyoto's cityscape. The main hall, built without the use of nails, juts out over a hillside, providing a breathtaking sight. Explore the temple's various pagodas, gardens, and sacred water spring, and learn about its historical and cultural significance.

Gion District:

Step into the world of geishas and traditional Japanese culture as you visit the historic Gion district. This atmospheric neighborhood is known for its preserved wooden machiya houses, teahouses, and traditional shops. Take a leisurely stroll along Hanamikoji Street, the main thoroughfare, and keep an eye out for geishas gracefully walking to their appointments. Enjoy a traditional tea ceremony, savor Kyoto's local delicacies, and soak in the ambiance of this timeless district.

Ryoan-ji Temple:

Discover the serene beauty of Ryoan-ji Temple, famous for its Zen rock garden. This minimalist garden features 15 carefully placed rocks surrounded by raked white gravel, creating a meditative space that encourages contemplation. Sit on the veranda and admire the simplicity and harmony of the garden, allowing your thoughts to flow freely.

Kinkaku-ji and Ginkaku-ji (Silver Pavilion):

End your exploration of Kyoto by visiting the Ginkaku-ji, also known as the Silver Pavilion. While not actually covered in silver, this temple is a masterpiece of Zen aesthetics. Explore the beautifully landscaped gardens, the iconic sand garden, and the picturesque moss-covered pond. Reflect on the tranquility of this peaceful place and appreciate the subtlety of its design.

Kyoto's ancient temples and tranquil gardens offer a glimpse into the rich cultural heritage of Japan. Immerse yourself in the beauty of this historic city, stroll through its charming neighborhoods, and embrace the serenity that permeates every corner. As you explore Kyoto's timeless treasures, you'll discover a profound sense of peace and a deeper appreciation for the traditions that have shaped Japan's identity.

Osaka: Food, Fun, and Urban Delights

Osaka, the lively and vibrant city in western Japan, is a captivating destination that entices travelers with its delectable cuisine, bustling streets, and vibrant nightlife. Known as the "Nation's Kitchen," Osaka is a culinary haven, offering a wide array of mouthwatering street food, local specialties, and Michelin-starred restaurants. In this chapter, we will delve into the exciting world of Osaka, exploring its culinary delights, cultural attractions, and urban adventures.

Dotonbori:

Begin your Osaka journey in the heart of the city at Dotonbori, a bustling entertainment district famous for its vibrant neon lights, larger-than-life signs, and energetic atmosphere. Take a stroll along the canal-lined street and immerse yourself in the sensory feast of sights, sounds, and smells. Indulge in local specialties like takoyaki (octopus balls), okonomiyaki (savory pancakes), and kushikatsu (deep-fried skewers). Don't forget to snap a photo with the iconic Glico Running Man sign, an emblem of Osaka's vibrant spirit.

Osaka Castle:

Step back in time as you visit Osaka Castle, a magnificent symbol of the city's history and resilience. This majestic castle, surrounded by beautiful gardens and moats, offers a glimpse into Japan's feudal past. Explore the castle's interior, which houses a museum showcasing the life and times of the samurai, and climb to the top for panoramic views of the city. During cherry blossom season, the castle grounds transform into a picturesque wonderland, attracting locals and tourists alike.

Universal Studios Japan:

For a day of family-friendly fun and entertainment, head to Universal Studios Japan (USJ). This world-renowned theme park features thrilling rides, live shows, and attractions based on popular movies and characters, such as Harry Potter, Jurassic Park, and Hello Kitty. Immerse yourself in the magical world of fantasy and adventure as you explore the various themed areas and enjoy exhilarating experiences.

Kuromon Ichiba Market:

Embark on a culinary adventure at Kuromon Ichiba Market, a paradise for food lovers. This bustling market is brimming with fresh seafood, local produce, and specialty shops offering a wide range of delicious treats. Sample regional delicacies like sushi, sashimi, oden (hot pot), and freshly grilled seafood. Engage with the friendly vendors, learn about the ingredients, and savor the authentic flavors that make Osaka's cuisine so renowned.

Sumiyoshi Taisha Shrine:

Discover the spiritual side of Osaka as you visit Sumiyoshi Taisha, one of Japan's oldest Shinto shrines. This serene and picturesque shrine, nestled among tall trees, is known for its unique architectural style and beautiful vermillion-colored buildings. Take a leisurely stroll through the grounds, cross the iconic Taiko-bashi Bridge, and experience the tranquility of this sacred place.

Shinsekai:

Experience the nostalgic charm of Shinsekai, a district that harkens back to Osaka's past. This vibrant neighborhood is characterized by its retro atmosphere, colorful signs, and bustling streets. Take a ride on the Tsutenkaku Tower for panoramic views, wander through the narrow streets lined with izakayas (traditional pubs) and street food stalls, and sample local favorites like kushikatsu and negiyaki (a savory pancake).

Osaka Aquarium Kaiyukan:

Delve into the wonders of the deep sea at Osaka Aquarium Kaiyukan, one of the largest aquariums in the world. This impressive facility showcases a diverse range of marine life, including giant whale sharks, playful dolphins, and colorful tropical fish. Walk through the mesmerizing tunnel surrounded by water, witness feeding sessions, and learn about the importance of marine conservation.

Osaka's vibrant street food culture, rich history, and modern attractions make it a city that offers something for everyone. Immerse yourself in the culinary delights, immerse yourself in the energetic atmosphere of Dotonbori, and experience the magic of Osaka's urban delights. As you indulge in the flavors and immerse yourself in the city's cultural offerings, you'll discover why Osaka is a destination that leaves a lasting impression on every traveler.

Hiroshima: A City of Peace and Resilience

Hiroshima, a city in western Japan, is known worldwide for its tragic history and remarkable resilience. Despite being devastated by the atomic bomb during World War II, Hiroshima has emerged as a symbol of peace and hope, showcasing the indomitable spirit of its people. In this chapter, we will explore the city's poignant memorials, vibrant culture, and serene beauty, while paying tribute to its journey from devastation to a beacon of peace.

Hiroshima Peace Memorial Park:

Begin your journey in Hiroshima at the Hiroshima Peace Memorial Park, a place of remembrance and reflection. This expansive park, located near the hypocenter of the atomic bomb explosion, houses several memorials and monuments dedicated to the victims of the bombing. Visit the iconic Atomic Bomb Dome, a UNESCO World Heritage site, which stands as a haunting reminder of the destructive power of nuclear weapons. Explore the Peace Memorial Museum, which provides a comprehensive account of the events surrounding the bombing and promotes a message of peace and nuclear disarmament.

Hiroshima Peace Memorial Museum:

Delve deeper into Hiroshima's history and the impact of the atomic bomb at the Hiroshima Peace Memorial Museum. The museum houses a collection of artifacts, photographs, and personal stories that offer a sobering glimpse into the tragedy and its aftermath. Learn about the lives of the victims, the city's recovery efforts, and the ongoing pursuit of nuclear disarmament. The museum serves as a testament to the resilience of the Hiroshima community and their commitment to promoting peace.

Shukkei-en Garden:

Find solace and tranquility in the serene beauty of Shukkei-en Garden. This traditional Japanese garden, located near the city center, offers a peaceful retreat from the urban bustle. Stroll along winding paths, admire the meticulously landscaped ponds, bridges, and teahouses, and enjoy the changing scenery with the seasons. Shukkei-en, which means "shrunken-scenery garden," showcases miniature landscapes inspired by famous natural scenes in Japan.

Miyajima Island:

A short ferry ride from Hiroshima takes you to the enchanting Miyajima Island. Known for its iconic floating torii gate, which appears to be floating on water during high tide, Miyajima is a place of natural beauty and cultural significance. Explore the Itsukushima Shrine, a UNESCO World Heritage site, and witness its stunning architecture and intricate details. Take a hike up Mount Misen for panoramic views of the Seto Inland Sea, visit the Miyajima Aquarium, and interact with the friendly local deer that roam freely on the island.

Hiroshima Castle:

Discover the rich samurai history of Hiroshima as you visit Hiroshima Castle, also known as Carp Castle. Although the original castle was destroyed in the atomic bombing, it has been meticulously reconstructed and now serves as a museum dedicated to the region's feudal past. Explore the castle's exhibits, admire the impressive architecture, and enjoy the views from the observation deck. Cherry blossom season transforms the castle grounds into a picturesque wonderland, attracting visitors from near and far.

Hiroshima Okonomiyaki:

No visit to Hiroshima is complete without indulging in its iconic dish, Hiroshima-style okonomiyaki. This savory pancake-like dish is made with layers of cabbage, noodles, meat, seafood, and a special okonomiyaki sauce. Watch as the skilled chefs prepare your okonomiyaki on a hot griddle, and savor the explosion of flavors and textures. Hiroshima is renowned for its vibrant food scene, so be sure to explore other local specialties such as Hiroshima-style tsukemen (dipping noodles) and oysters.

Mazda Museum:

For automotive enthusiasts, a visit to the Mazda Museum is a must. Hiroshima is the birthplace of Mazda, one of Japan's leading automobile manufacturers. Immerse yourself in the world of Mazda as you explore interactive exhibits, learn about the company's history and innovative technologies, and see a collection of iconic Mazda vehicles.

Hiroshima's journey from devastation to a city of peace and resilience is a testament to the strength of the human spirit. By visiting Hiroshima, you pay homage to the past, gain a deeper understanding of the consequences of war, and embrace the city's message of peace and hope. Through its memorials, cultural treasures, and warm hospitality, Hiroshima leaves an indelible mark on all who visit, reminding us of the importance of compassion, forgiveness, and a world free from nuclear weapons.

Hokkaido: Nature's Wonderland in the North

Hokkaido, the northernmost island of Japan, is a captivating destination renowned for its pristine landscapes, abundant wildlife, and unique cultural experiences. Known as a nature lover's paradise, Hokkaido offers a wide array of outdoor activities, from exploring national parks and soaking in hot springs to indulging in fresh seafood and witnessing the stunning beauty of its seasons. In this chapter, we will embark on a journey through Hokkaido's breathtaking wonders and discover the magic of this untamed wilderness.

Sapporo:

Begin your Hokkaido adventure in Sapporo, the vibrant capital city. Famous for its annual snow festival and delicious local cuisine, Sapporo offers a mix of urban attractions and natural beauty. Explore Odori Park, a long, green oasis in the heart of the city, and visit the Sapporo Clock Tower, a symbol of Sapporo's history. Indulge in a bowl of piping hot miso ramen, a local specialty, and enjoy the lively atmosphere of Susukino, Sapporo's entertainment district.

Furano and Biei:

Immerse yourself in the picturesque landscapes of Furano and Biei, known for their rolling hills, colorful flower fields, and charming rural scenery. Visit Furano Flower Fields during the summer months, when lavender, poppies, and other vibrant blooms create a stunning tapestry of colors. In Biei, explore the Patchwork Road, a scenic route dotted with picturesque fields, tree-lined roads, and quaint farmhouses. The beauty of these regions has made them popular settings for many Japanese films and commercials.

Shiretoko National Park:

Venture into the wild beauty of Shiretoko National Park, a UNESCO World Heritage site and one of Japan's last remaining untouched wilderness areas. This remote and rugged region is home to diverse ecosystems, including dense forests, towering cliffs, and pristine lakes. Take a boat tour to explore the park's dramatic coastline, keep an eye out for wildlife such as brown bears and red foxes, and witness the breathtaking sight of the Shiretoko Five Lakes.

Noboribetsu Onsen:

Indulge in the therapeutic relaxation of Noboribetsu Onsen, one of Japan's most famous hot spring resorts. Nestled in a volcanic valley, Noboribetsu offers a rejuvenating experience with its numerous hot spring baths and foot baths. Soak in the mineral-rich waters, believed to have healing properties, and immerse yourself in the serene ambiance of this natural spa town. Don't miss the spectacular sight of the Jigokudani (Hell Valley), a geothermal valley with steaming vents and sulfurous fumes.

Otaru:

Experience the charm of Otaru, a historic port city known for its beautifully preserved canal district and glassworks. Stroll along the canal, lined with 19th-century warehouses that have been converted into shops, cafes, and museums. Visit the Otaru Music Box Museum, where you can browse through a vast collection of intricately crafted music boxes. Indulge in the city's fresh seafood, especially the renowned Otaru sushi and seafood bowls.

Lake Toya:

Discover the tranquility of Lake Toya, a volcanic caldera lake surrounded by picturesque mountains. Take a leisurely cruise on the lake, soak in hot spring baths overlooking the water, and savor the local delicacies, including the famous Toyako-ko Manju (steamed buns filled with sweet bean paste). For breathtaking views, ride the Mount Usu Ropeway and marvel at the panoramic vistas of the lake and the volcanic landscapes.

Hokkaido Wildlife:

Hokkaido is a haven for wildlife enthusiasts, offering opportunities to spot rare and majestic creatures. In the winter, head to Rausu in the eastern part of the island for a chance to observe the magnificent Steller's sea eagles, white-tailed eagles, and other seabirds. In the summer, visit the Kushiro Marshland, a designated national park and a crucial habitat for endangered species like the red-crowned crane. Take a boat tour to glimpse these elegant birds dancing in their natural habitat.

Hokkaido's natural wonders, unique culture, and welcoming atmosphere make it a destination that captures the hearts of travelers. Whether you seek outdoor adventures, cultural experiences, or simply a peaceful retreat surrounded by nature, Hokkaido offers an abundance of opportunities to create unforgettable memories. As you explore its untamed wilderness, you'll come to understand why Hokkaido is often referred to as "Nature's Wonderland in the North."

Nara: The Land of Sacred Deer and Historic Temples

Nara, a small city located in the Kansai region of Japan, is a treasure trove of ancient history, cultural heritage, and natural beauty. As the capital of Japan during the Nara period (710-794), it holds significant historical importance and is home to some of the country's oldest and most revered temples. In this chapter, we will delve into the captivating world of Nara, exploring its iconic landmarks, friendly sacred deer, and the profound spiritual atmosphere that permeates the city.

Nara Park:

Begin your journey in Nara Park, a vast expanse of greenery that serves as the centerpiece of the city. This expansive park is famous for its free-roaming deer, considered sacred messengers of the gods in Shinto belief. Interact with these gentle creatures, feed them special deer crackers (shika senbei), and capture unforgettable moments. The park is also home to several key attractions, including the iconic Todai-ji Temple and Kasuga Taisha Shrine.

Todai-ji Temple:

Marvel at the grandeur of Todai-ji Temple, one of Japan's most significant Buddhist temples and a UNESCO World Heritage site. The temple houses the awe-inspiring Great Buddha (Daibutsu), a colossal bronze statue of Buddha that stands at over 15 meters tall. Step inside the Great Buddha Hall (Daibutsuden), the largest wooden building in the world, and immerse yourself in the spiritual ambiance as you witness this magnificent masterpiece.

Kasuga Taisha Shrine:

Step into the mystical world of Kasuga Taisha Shrine, an important Shinto shrine known for its thousands of stone and bronze lanterns lining the paths. The shrine's vibrant vermilion-colored buildings, intricate carvings, and tranquil forested surroundings create a captivating atmosphere. Visit during the Setsubun Mantoro Festival in February, when the lanterns are lit, casting an ethereal glow throughout the shrine.

Horyu-ji Temple:

Embark on a journey to Horyu-ji Temple, a sacred site that dates back to the 7th century and is recognized as one of the world's oldest wooden structures. This temple complex comprises several buildings, including the iconic pagoda, which stands as a testament to the architectural brilliance of ancient Japan. Explore the treasure house (Hokki-kan), which houses an extensive collection of Buddhist statues, scriptures, and artifacts.

Nara National Museum:

Delve into Nara's rich cultural heritage at the Nara National Museum, an institution dedicated to preserving and showcasing Japan's artistic treasures. The museum exhibits a wide range of Buddhist sculptures, paintings, calligraphy, and decorative arts, providing insight into the artistic and spiritual legacy of the region. Don't miss the opportunity to admire the museum's seasonal exhibitions, which highlight different aspects of Japanese art and culture.

Yoshiki-en Garden:

Experience the serenity of Yoshiki-en Garden, a hidden gem tucked away behind Nara's main temples. This traditional Japanese garden features meticulously landscaped ponds, stone lanterns, and lush vegetation. Take a leisurely stroll along the winding paths, breathe in the fragrant scents of flowers and trees, and find moments of tranquility amidst the bustling city.

Isuien Garden:

Immerse yourself in the beauty of Isuien Garden, a historic garden that seamlessly combines two distinct styles: a traditional Japanese garden and a more modern garden with Western influences. Explore the garden's diverse landscapes, including ponds, streams, and tea houses, and admire the seasonal beauty of cherry blossoms in spring and vibrant foliage in autumn.

Nara's blend of history, nature, and spirituality creates a captivating atmosphere that leaves a lasting impression on visitors. As you wander through the ancient temples, interact with the sacred deer, and immerse yourself in the city's cultural treasures, you'll come to appreciate Nara as a true testament to Japan's rich heritage.

Hakone and Mount Fuji: Majestic Beauty and Hot Springs

Hakone, nestled in the Fuji-Hakone-Izu National Park, is a renowned destination in Japan known for its stunning natural landscapes, breathtaking views of Mount Fuji, and relaxing hot springs. Located just a short distance from Tokyo, Hakone offers a tranquil escape from the bustling city life, inviting travelers to immerse themselves in the majestic beauty of the region. In this chapter, we will embark on a journey through Hakone and explore the allure of its landscapes, the iconic Mount Fuji, and the rejuvenating hot springs.

Mount Fuji:

No visit to Hakone would be complete without encountering the awe-inspiring Mount Fuji, Japan's highest peak and a symbol of the country's natural beauty. On a clear day, the view of Mount Fuji from various vantage points in Hakone is simply breathtaking. Take a boat cruise on Lake Ashi and witness the iconic image of Mount Fuji reflected in the tranquil waters. Alternatively, ride the Hakone Ropeway or the Komagatake Ropeway for a panoramic view of the mountain and the surrounding landscapes.

Hakone Open-Air Museum:

Immerse yourself in the world of art at the Hakone Open-Air Museum, a unique outdoor museum showcasing contemporary sculptures and artworks against the backdrop of nature. Explore the expansive sculpture park, featuring works by renowned artists from around the world. Admire the fusion of art and nature as you stroll through the beautifully landscaped gardens and discover the impressive collection of sculptures, including works by Picasso and Rodin.

Hakone Shrine:

Visit the iconic Hakone Shrine, a Shinto shrine nestled on the shores of Lake Ashi. The shrine's picturesque red torii gate, partially submerged in the lake, creates a mesmerizing scene. Take a leisurely walk along the cedar-lined path leading to the main hall, where you can offer prayers and immerse yourself in the peaceful ambiance. The shrine is particularly enchanting during the autumn months when the surrounding trees are ablaze with vibrant colors.

Owakudani:

Embark on a thrilling adventure to Owakudani, a volcanic valley known for its active sulfurous vents and hot springs. Take a scenic cable car ride to reach this otherworldly destination, and be greeted by the pungent smell of sulfur and the sight of steaming fumaroles. Explore the area's walking trails, sample black eggs boiled in the naturally hot mineral-rich waters (said to add years to your life), and marvel at the panoramic views of the surrounding volcanic landscape.

Hakone Ropeway:

Embark on a breathtaking journey aboard the Hakone Ropeway, a cable car system that traverses the volcanic valleys and lush forests of Hakone. As you ascend, you'll be treated to stunning vistas of Mount Fuji, Lake Ashi, and the surrounding landscapes. Make sure to have your camera ready to capture the awe-inspiring panoramic views from the ropeway.

Hakone Onsen:

Indulge in the ultimate relaxation experience by soaking in the hot springs, or onsen, for which Hakone is famous. The region boasts numerous traditional ryokans (Japanese inns) and resorts that offer luxurious hot spring baths with picturesque views. Immerse yourself in the therapeutic waters, believed to have healing properties, and unwind amidst the serene natural surroundings. Whether you choose a public bath or a private open-air bath, the tranquil atmosphere and rejuvenating properties of the hot springs will leave you feeling refreshed and rejuvenated.

Hakone Museum of Art:

Appreciate the beauty of Japanese art at the Hakone Museum of Art, a hidden gem nestled in a tranquil garden. This museum specializes in showcasing the works of famous Japanese painters and ceramic artists, with a focus on traditional Japanese art forms such as ink painting and tea ceremony ceramics. Explore the carefully curated exhibitions, stroll through the peaceful gardens, and gain a deeper appreciation for the intricacies of Japanese art and culture.

Hakone and Mount Fuji offer a captivating blend of natural beauty, cultural experiences, and serene relaxation. Whether you're seeking adventure, artistic inspiration, or a tranquil escape, Hakone's majestic landscapes and rejuvenating hot springs will undoubtedly leave a lasting impression on your journey through Japan.

Traditional Japanese Cuisine: Sushi, Ramen, and More

Japanese cuisine is celebrated worldwide for its artful presentation, exquisite flavors, and emphasis on fresh, seasonal ingredients. From delicate sushi rolls to savory bowls of ramen, Japan's culinary traditions have captured the hearts and taste buds of food enthusiasts around the globe. In this chapter, we will delve into the diverse world of traditional Japanese cuisine, exploring iconic dishes, regional specialties, and the unique culinary experiences that await you on your journey through Japan.

Sushi:

Sushi, perhaps the most iconic Japanese dish, showcases the harmony of flavors and textures that Japanese cuisine is renowned for. Made with vinegared rice and a variety of toppings, including fresh fish, seafood, and vegetables, sushi offers a delightful culinary experience. Whether you indulge in nigiri sushi (hand-pressed rice topped with fish) or maki sushi (rolled sushi wrapped in seaweed), be sure to visit a sushiya (sushi restaurant) to savor the authentic flavors and meticulous craftsmanship.

Ramen:

No visit to Japan is complete without trying a steaming bowl of ramen. This soul-warming dish features wheat noodles served in a flavorful broth, accompanied by an array of toppings such as sliced pork, green onions, nori (seaweed), and a soft-boiled egg. Each region in Japan boasts its own unique style of ramen, from the rich and creamy tonkotsu ramen of Hakata to the soy-based shoyu ramen of Tokyo. Explore the local ramen shops, known as ramen-ya, to sample the regional variations and discover your favorite bowl.

Tempura:

Tempura is a beloved Japanese dish consisting of lightly battered and deep-fried seafood, vegetables, and sometimes even sweets. The batter used in tempura is often made with a delicate mix of flour, water, and sometimes egg, resulting in a crispy and airy texture. Savor the contrast between the crispy exterior and the tender interior as you enjoy tempura prawns, vegetables like sweet potato and eggplant, and seasonal seafood.

Sashimi:

For seafood lovers, sashimi is a must-try delicacy. Sashimi showcases the purity and freshness of raw fish or seafood, expertly sliced and served without any additional seasoning or cooking. Popular types of sashimi include maguro (tuna), salmon, hamachi (yellowtail), and tako (octopus). Enjoy the subtle flavors and smooth textures of these pristine seafood offerings, accompanied by soy sauce and wasabi for an added kick.

Kaiseki:

Embark on a gastronomic journey through the refined world of kaiseki, a traditional multi-course dining experience that showcases the essence of

Japanese culinary artistry. Rooted in the tea ceremony tradition, kaiseki is a meticulously crafted meal consisting of several small dishes, each thoughtfully prepared and beautifully presented. The dishes highlight seasonal ingredients and are designed to create a harmonious balance of flavors, textures, and colors. Indulging in a kaiseki meal is a true culinary adventure, allowing you to appreciate the intricacies of Japanese cuisine.

Izakaya:

Immerse yourself in the lively atmosphere of an izakaya, a type of informal Japanese pub where friends gather to enjoy drinks and a wide variety of small plates known as "izakaya food." Izakayas offer a diverse selection of dishes, including yakitori (grilled skewered chicken), gyoza (dumplings), karaage (deep-fried chicken), and edamame (boiled soybeans). Pair these delectable bites with a glass of sake or a cold beer, and relish the conviviality of this popular Japanese dining style.

Wagyu Beef:

Indulge in the melt-in-your-mouth luxury of wagyu beef, renowned for its exceptional marbling and tender texture. Japan is home to several varieties of wagyu, with Kobe beef being the most famous. Treat yourself to a mouthwatering wagyu steak or experience the art of shabu-shabu, where thin slices of wagyu are briefly dipped in hot broth before being savored with dipping sauces.

Japanese cuisine offers a world of culinary delights, from the simplicity and elegance of sushi to the comforting warmth of ramen. As you explore Japan, be sure to sample the regional specialties, dine at local establishments, and embrace the culture of food appreciation that is deeply ingrained in Japanese society. Your taste buds will thank you for the unforgettable culinary experiences that await you on your journey through Japan.

Izakayas and Nightlife: Enjoying the Japanese Pub Culture

Japan's vibrant nightlife scene offers a kaleidoscope of experiences, from the energetic streets of Tokyo to the historic alleys of Kyoto. At the heart of Japanese nightlife is the izakaya, a type of informal pub where locals and visitors gather to socialize, enjoy delicious food, and partake in a wide array of beverages. In this chapter, we will dive into the captivating world of izakayas and explore the diverse facets of Japan's vibrant nightlife, inviting you to embrace the spirited atmosphere and create unforgettable memories.

What is an Izakaya?

An izakaya is a casual and lively establishment where people come to unwind after work, socialize with friends, and enjoy a wide range of food and drinks. These establishments typically have an extensive menu featuring a variety of small plates, known as "izakaya food," which pair well with alcoholic beverages. Izakayas are known for their convivial ambiance, making them the perfect place to experience the Japanese pub culture and mingle with locals.

Izakaya Food:

The food served at izakayas is a delightful exploration of flavors and textures. From yakitori (grilled skewered chicken) to karaage (deep-fried chicken), gyoza (dumplings) to takoyaki (octopus balls), the izakaya menu offers a diverse selection of dishes to satisfy every palate. Don't miss out on classic favorites like edamame (boiled soybeans), agedashi tofu (deep-fried tofu in a savory sauce), and sashimi (fresh raw fish). Explore the menu, try a variety of dishes, and let your taste buds embark on a culinary adventure.

Sake:

No visit to an izakaya is complete without trying Japan's iconic rice wine, sake. Sake is deeply ingrained in Japanese culture and has a rich history that spans centuries. Izakayas often have an extensive selection of sake, ranging from dry to sweet, and from light to full-bodied. Explore different types and flavors of sake, and appreciate the craftsmanship and tradition that goes into producing this beloved beverage.

Shochu and Awamori:

For those looking to explore other traditional Japanese spirits, izakayas also offer shochu and awamori. Shochu is a distilled liquor typically made from barley, rice, sweet potatoes, or other ingredients, and it can be enjoyed on its own or mixed with various drinks. Awamori, on the other hand, is a unique spirit from Okinawa made from long-grain indica rice. These spirits offer a different drinking experience and are worth sampling for those seeking a taste of Japanese alcohol beyond sake.

Craft Beer:

Japan's craft beer scene has experienced a surge in popularity in recent years, and many izakayas now offer a wide selection of locally brewed craft beers. From pale ales to stouts, lagers to IPAs, craft beer enthusiasts will find a diverse range of flavors and styles to enjoy. Explore the izakaya's craft beer menu and savor the unique brews, often made with local ingredients and showcasing the creativity of Japan's burgeoning craft beer industry.

Karaoke:

Karaoke is a beloved pastime in Japan, and many izakayas offer private karaoke rooms where you can sing your heart out with friends or fellow patrons. Belt out your favorite tunes, indulge in some lively group singing, and embrace the fun and festive atmosphere of karaoke. It's a great way to immerse yourself in Japanese pop culture and create memorable moments of laughter and camaraderie.

Golden Gai and Piss Alley:

For a taste of Tokyo's historic nightlife, venture into the narrow alleys of Golden Gai in Shinjuku or Piss Alley (also known as Omoide Yokocho) in Shibuya. These atmospheric districts are packed with tiny bars and eateries, each with its own unique charm. Experience the nostalgic ambiance, chat with friendly locals and fellow travelers, and savor the intimate setting of these hidden gems. Golden Gai and Piss Alley offer a glimpse into the bygone era of Tokyo's nightlife and are perfect for those seeking a more intimate and authentic izakaya experience.

Immerse yourself in the spirited atmosphere of

izakayas and embrace the excitement of Japan's nightlife. Whether you're enjoying a delicious plate of yakitori, sipping on sake, or singing your heart out at karaoke, the izakaya culture offers a vibrant and unforgettable experience that captures the essence of Japanese hospitality and camaraderie. Cheers to a memorable night out in Japan!

Onsen (Hot Springs) Experience: Relaxation and Rejuvenation

Japan is renowned for its therapeutic hot springs, known as onsens, which have been cherished for centuries for their healing properties and rejuvenating effects. From luxurious resort spas to rustic mountain retreats, onsen experiences offer a blissful escape from the hustle and bustle of everyday life. In this chapter, we will immerse ourselves in the world of onsens, exploring their cultural significance, health benefits, and the etiquette that surrounds these serene havens of relaxation.

What is an Onsen?

Onsens are natural hot springs that are abundant throughout Japan, thanks to the country's geothermal activity. The mineral-rich waters of onsens are believed to have numerous health benefits, including soothing muscle aches, promoting circulation, and relieving stress. Onsens can be found in various settings, from indoor baths in modern facilities to outdoor pools nestled in breathtaking natural landscapes.

Cultural Significance of Onsens:

Onsens hold a special place in Japanese culture and are deeply ingrained in the daily lives of many Japanese people. They are not only seen as a place for physical rejuvenation but also as a space for spiritual cleansing and relaxation. Onsen visits often follow specific rituals and customs that reflect the respect and appreciation for nature and communal bathing.

Types of Onsens:

There are several types of onsens, each offering a unique experience. Public onsens, known as "soto-yu," are communal bathing facilities that can be found in towns and cities. These onsens are a great opportunity to immerse yourself in the local culture and interact with the locals. Ryokans, traditional Japanese inns, often feature private onsens that can be enjoyed by guests staying at the inn. Some ryokans also have shared onsens for communal bathing. Additionally, there are mixed-gender onsens, where bathing attire is required, allowing visitors to enjoy the hot springs together.

Onsen Etiquette:

When visiting an onsen, it's important to be mindful of the etiquette to ensure a respectful and enjoyable experience for all. Before entering the bathing area, it is customary to wash your body thoroughly in the shower area. Tattoos are sometimes seen as a taboo in Japanese culture, so be aware that some onsens may have specific rules regarding tattoos. It's also essential to respect others' privacy and maintain a quiet and peaceful atmosphere within the bathing area.

Outdoor Onsens (Rotenburo):

One of the highlights of visiting an onsen is the opportunity to soak in an outdoor hot spring, known as a rotenburo. These open-air baths allow you to connect with nature while enjoying the soothing hot waters. Whether nestled in the mountains, overlooking a serene river, or surrounded by lush forests, rotenburo experiences offer a serene and picturesque setting that enhances the overall sense of relaxation.

Onsen Towns and Resorts:

Throughout Japan, there are numerous onsen towns and resorts that cater to those seeking a complete immersion in the onsen experience. Places like Hakone, Beppu, and Kusatsu are renowned for their onsen culture and offer a range of accommodations, from traditional ryokans to luxurious spa resorts. Exploring these onsen destinations allows you to fully embrace the tranquil ambiance and indulge in rejuvenating treatments and therapies.

Onsen Health Benefits:

Besides the relaxing and soothing effects, onsens are believed to offer various health benefits. The mineral-rich waters can alleviate conditions such as arthritis, skin ailments, and respiratory issues. The therapeutic properties of onsens have attracted visitors seeking natural remedies for their ailments for centuries. Immerse yourself in the warm waters and let the healing properties of the onsen envelop you.

Onsen Cuisine:

Many onsen towns and resorts offer delicious local cuisine that complements the onsen experience. Known as "Kaiseki Ryori," these multi-course meals feature seasonal and locally sourced ingredients. Indulge in fresh seafood, traditional vegetables, and delectable regional specialties, all prepared with meticulous attention to detail. Enjoying a Kaiseki Ryori meal after a soothing onsen bath adds an extra layer of culinary delight to your overall relaxation experience.

Visiting an onsen in Japan is not just about soaking in hot water—it's a holistic experience that combines relaxation, cultural immersion, and wellness. Whether you choose to unwind in a luxurious resort spa or seek solitude in a secluded mountain onsen, the tranquility and rejuvenation you'll find in the healing waters will leave you refreshed and invigorated. Allow yourself to surrender to the serenity of the onsen and embrace the therapeutic embrace of these natural wonders.

Japanese Tea Ceremony: A Window into Zen Culture

The Japanese tea ceremony, known as "chado" or "sado," is a centuries-old ritual that offers a profound glimpse into the essence of Zen culture. Rooted in simplicity, mindfulness, and hospitality, the tea ceremony is a meticulously choreographed performance that encompasses much more than the act of drinking tea. In this chapter, we will explore the beauty, significance, and rituals of the Japanese tea ceremony, inviting you to immerse yourself in this serene and meditative practice.

The Way of Tea:

The Japanese tea ceremony is often referred to as "chado" or "sado," which translates to "the way of tea." It is a spiritual and cultural practice that traces its origins back to the 9th century and is deeply influenced by Zen Buddhism. The tea ceremony embodies principles such as harmony, respect, purity, and tranquility, which are fundamental to the Zen philosophy.

Tea Houses:

The tea ceremony takes place in a traditional tea house, known as a "chashitsu." These small, intimate spaces are designed to create an atmosphere of tranquility and simplicity, allowing participants to fully engage in the tea ceremony experience. The architecture, interior design, and surrounding gardens of the tea house are carefully curated to enhance the sense of harmony with nature.

Tea Ceremony Utensils:

The tea ceremony is characterized by the use of specific utensils, each carefully selected for its aesthetic and functional qualities. The main utensils include the tea bowl (chawan), tea scoop (chashaku), tea whisk (chasen), and water kettle (kama). These items are often cherished heirlooms and hold symbolic significance in the tea ceremony.

Matcha: The Green Tea Powder:

Central to the Japanese tea ceremony is the preparation and consumption of matcha, a powdered green tea. Matcha is made from shade-grown tea leaves that are ground into a fine powder. The tea master (chajin) uses precise techniques to whisk the matcha with hot water, creating a frothy and vibrant green beverage. The flavor of matcha is distinctively rich and complex, and its consumption is considered a form of meditation.

Rituals and Etiquette:

The tea ceremony follows a series of precise rituals and etiquette, which participants are expected to observe. From the proper way to enter the tea house to the way tea utensils are handled and tea is served, each step of the ceremony is imbued with symbolism and meaning. The rituals and etiquette reflect the ideals of mindfulness, humility, and respect.

Zen Aesthetics:

The tea ceremony embraces the concept of

"wabi-sabi," which celebrates the beauty of imperfection and impermanence. The tea utensils and the tea house itself often exhibit simple and rustic designs, emphasizing natural materials and subtle beauty. The appreciation of imperfections, such as cracks in the tea bowl or the fleeting beauty of seasonal flowers, encourages participants to cultivate a sense of mindfulness and acceptance of the transient nature of life.

Tea Ceremony as a Cultural Experience:

Participating in a tea ceremony offers a unique opportunity to immerse oneself in Japanese culture and gain insights into the Zen philosophy. Many tea houses welcome visitors and offer tea ceremony experiences, allowing guests to witness the grace and precision of the tea master and partake in the ritual themselves. Engaging in a tea ceremony provides a deep connection to Japan's historical traditions and an appreciation for the pursuit of harmony and mindfulness.

The Japanese tea ceremony is a profound and meditative practice that invites participants to slow down, find inner calm, and appreciate the beauty of simplicity. As you engage in this time-honored ritual, allow yourself to be present in the moment, savor the flavors of matcha, and embrace the tranquility that surrounds you. The tea ceremony is not merely a beverage; it is a gateway to a deeper understanding of Japanese culture and the pursuit of a more harmonious way of life.

Geisha and Maiko: The Art of Traditional Entertainment

The world of geisha and maiko in Japan is a captivating and enigmatic aspect of traditional Japanese culture. With their elegant attire, impeccable manners, and mastery of traditional performing arts, geisha and maiko are not only symbols of beauty but also guardians of tradition and refined entertainment. In this chapter, we will delve into the enchanting world of geisha and maiko, exploring their history, training, distinctive appearances, and the significance they hold in Japanese society.

Geisha and Maiko: An Introduction:

Geisha and maiko are female entertainers who specialize in traditional Japanese arts such as music, dance, singing, and storytelling. While geisha are experienced professionals, maiko are apprentices who undergo years of training before becoming fully-fledged geisha. Together, they represent the epitome of grace, beauty, and cultural preservation.

Historical Background:

The tradition of geisha dates back to the Edo period (1603-1868), where they initially emerged as skilled performers and companions to samurai. Over time, geisha evolved into artists and entertainers who captivated audiences with their refined skills. Today, geisha and maiko continue to preserve this ancient tradition, showcasing the elegance and artistry of Japan's cultural heritage.

Training and Apprenticeship:

Becoming a geisha or maiko requires years of dedicated training. Young women, usually in their teens, enter an okiya (geisha house) and become maiko apprentices. Under the guidance of experienced geisha, they learn various arts such as traditional dance, playing musical instruments like the shamisen, tea ceremony, and the art of conversation. The training period can last for several years, during which maiko undergo a transformation in appearance and acquire the refined skills necessary to become geisha.

The Geisha Appearance:

The geisha and maiko's iconic appearance is instantly recognizable. Adorned in elaborate kimonos with vibrant patterns and intricate obis (sashes), their hairstyles are meticulously crafted with special combs, ornaments, and even real flowers. Their faces are painted in a distinctive manner, using white powder to create a porcelain-like complexion, accentuated by red and black accents for the lips and eyes. The attire and appearance of geisha and maiko represent the pinnacle of elegance and traditional beauty.

Traditional Arts and Entertainment:

Geisha and maiko are skilled in various traditional arts, which they showcase during performances known as ozashiki or banquet events. They entertain guests with dance, music, games, and witty conversation. The geisha's role is to create a sophisticated and engaging atmosphere, ensuring that guests have an enjoyable and memorable experience.

The Geisha World:

The geisha world is a tightly-knit community with its own hierarchy and customs. Geisha and maiko are associated with specific districts, such as Kyoto's Gion or Tokyo's Asakusa, where they entertain guests in exclusive teahouses and ochaya (tea houses). These establishments provide a glimpse into the secretive world of geisha, offering a unique and immersive experience for those fortunate enough to be invited.

Geisha and Maiko Today:

In modern times, the number of geisha and maiko has significantly declined, and their role has shifted more towards cultural preservation and tourism. Geisha and maiko performances are highly sought after, particularly by visitors who wish to witness the grace and skill of these remarkable artists. Some teahouses and cultural centers offer opportunities for interactions and performances, allowing guests to appreciate the beauty and artistry of geisha and maiko.

Respect and Etiquette:

When encountering geisha or maiko, it is essential to observe proper etiquette and respect their privacy. Taking photographs without permission or approaching them inappropriately is considered disrespectful. It is best to appreciate their artistry and presence from a distance, understanding the historical and cultural significance they represent.

The world of geisha and maiko is a mesmerizing realm that bridges the past with the present, showcasing the elegance, artistry, and dedication to preserving Japan's cultural heritage. Their performances and presence evoke a sense of grace and refinement, offering a glimpse into a bygone era. Witnessing the artistry of geisha and maiko is a truly remarkable experience, allowing visitors to embrace the enchanting beauty of traditional Japanese entertainment.

Sumo Wrestling: Witness the Ancient Sport

Sumo wrestling is a time-honored tradition in Japan, steeped in history, ritual, and the sheer power of its participants. This chapter invites you to delve into the fascinating world of sumo wrestling, exploring its origins, rules, rituals, and the unparalleled experience of witnessing this ancient sport firsthand.

The Origins of Sumo:

Sumo wrestling has deep roots in Japanese culture, tracing back over 1,500 years. It is believed to have originated as a religious ritual dedicated to appeasing the Shinto gods and ensuring bountiful harvests. Over time, sumo evolved into a competitive sport, combining physical strength, technique, and mental discipline.

Sumo Rules and Regulations:

Sumo matches take place in a circular ring called a dohyo. The objective is simple: force your opponent out of the ring or make them touch the ground with any part of their body other than the soles of their feet. Matches are short but intense, often lasting only a few seconds. The rules and rituals surrounding sumo add to the intrigue and allure of this ancient sport.

The Yokozuna: The Highest Rank:

The pinnacle of sumo wrestling is the rank of yokozuna. Yokozuna are the grand champions, considered the embodiment of sumo's ideals. They are revered for their skill, strength, and adherence to traditional values. The promotion to yokozuna is a rare and prestigious honor, achieved by only a select few throughout history.

Sumo Stables:

Sumo wrestlers live and train together in communal facilities known as sumo stables or heya. These stables serve as a home, training ground, and support system for the wrestlers. Visitors can catch a glimpse of the wrestlers' daily routines and witness their rigorous training sessions, providing a unique insight into their disciplined lifestyle.

The Sumo Wrestler's Diet:

Sumo wrestlers follow a strict diet known as chankonabe to maintain their impressive physiques. Chankonabe is a hearty and nutritious stew consisting of meat, fish, vegetables, and tofu. The high-calorie and protein-rich nature of this traditional dish fuels the wrestlers' intense training and helps them build the strength required for their bouts.

Sumo Tournaments:

Sumo tournaments, known as basho, are held six times a year in various locations across Japan. These tournaments attract thousands of spectators, both locals and tourists, who come to witness the fierce clashes and displays of athleticism. Each basho spans 15 days, with wrestlers competing against different opponents to climb the ranks and earn recognition.

The Spectacle of Sumo:

Attending a sumo tournament is an awe-inspiring experience. The atmosphere is electric as the crowd erupts with excitement during intense matches. Witnessing the wrestlers' size, agility, and raw power up close is truly captivating. The rituals, such as the ceremonial stomping of feet and salt-throwing, add a touch of mystique to the proceedings.

The Cultural Significance:

Sumo wrestling embodies traditional Japanese values such as discipline, respect, and perseverance. It serves as a symbol of national pride and cultural identity. Beyond its sporting aspect, sumo reflects the deep-rooted traditions, rituals, and aesthetics that are inherent in Japanese society.

Visiting a sumo tournament provides a rare glimpse into the ancient world of this captivating sport. The thunderous applause, the intensity of the matches, and the palpable energy within the arena create an unforgettable experience. Whether you are a sports enthusiast or simply intrigued by Japanese culture, witnessing sumo wrestling is a must-do when exploring the Land of the Rising Sun.

Manga and Anime: The World of Japanese Pop Culture

When it comes to Japanese pop culture, manga and anime are at the forefront, captivating audiences around the globe with their unique storytelling, vibrant artwork, and diverse characters. This chapter delves into the fascinating world of manga and anime, exploring their origins, impact on popular culture, and the immersive experiences they offer to fans.

Manga: The Art of Japanese Comics:

Manga refers to Japanese comic books and graphic novels, which are renowned for their distinct artistic style and engaging narratives. Originating in the late 19th century, manga has evolved into a vast and diverse medium, covering a wide range of genres such as action, romance, fantasy, science fiction, and more. Its popularity extends beyond Japan, with manga being translated and enjoyed by fans worldwide.

Anime: Animated Delights:

Anime refers to Japanese animated productions, which bring manga stories to life through captivating visuals and compelling storytelling. Anime covers a vast array of genres and themes, ranging from epic adventures and fantastical worlds to slice-of-life dramas and thought-provoking narratives. With its unique animation styles and immersive storytelling techniques, anime has become a global phenomenon, capturing the hearts of fans across different cultures.

Origins and Influences:

Manga and anime draw inspiration from Japan's rich artistic traditions, such as ukiyo-e woodblock prints and traditional storytelling formats like kabuki and Noh theater. Additionally, Western influences, particularly from American comics and animation, have also played a significant role in shaping the style and content of manga and anime. The fusion of these diverse influences has contributed to the distinctive and globally appealing nature of Japanese pop culture.

Iconic Manga and Anime:

Japanese manga and anime have produced numerous iconic series that have achieved international acclaim. From classics like "Astro Boy" and "Dragon Ball" to modern favorites like "One Piece" and "Attack on Titan," these titles have captivated audiences with their memorable characters, immersive worlds, and compelling narratives. The enduring popularity of these series reflects the broad appeal and impact of manga and anime on popular culture.

Cosplay: Embodying Characters:

Cosplay, short for "costume play," is a phenomenon deeply rooted in manga and anime culture. It involves fans dressing up as their favorite manga or anime characters, meticulously recreating their costumes and embodying their mannerisms. Cosplay has become an integral part of conventions and events worldwide, allowing fans to express their creativity, connect with fellow enthusiasts, and celebrate their love for manga and anime.

Manga Cafés and Anime Stores:

In Japan, manga cafés, known as manga kissa, offer a unique experience for fans to immerse themselves in the world of manga. These cafés provide comfortable reading spaces with extensive manga collections, allowing visitors to browse, read, and enjoy their favorite titles for hours. Additionally, anime stores offer a wide range of merchandise, including figurines, posters, DVDs, and other collectibles, providing fans with an opportunity to bring their favorite characters home.

Studio Visits and Theme Parks:

Visiting anime studios or theme parks dedicated to popular manga and anime series can be an exciting and immersive experience. Studio tours offer a behind-the-scenes look at the animation process, showcasing the intricate work involved in bringing characters and stories to life. Theme parks, such as the Ghibli Museum or Universal Studios Japan's anime attractions, allow fans to step into the worlds of their beloved series and indulge in interactive experiences.

Cultural Impact and Global Appeal:

Manga and anime have had a profound impact on popular culture, influencing not only entertainment but also fashion, music, gaming, and even tourism. The global popularity of manga and anime has led to the establishment of dedicated conventions, fan communities, and even academic studies exploring the cultural significance and artistic value of these mediums.

Immersing oneself in the world of manga and anime is an essential part of exploring Japanese pop culture. Whether you are a long-time fan or a newcomer to this vibrant world, manga and anime offer a diverse range of stories, captivating artwork, and immersive experiences that will leave you enthralled and eager for more. So, dive into the pages of a manga or embark on an anime binge-watching session, and let the magic of Japanese pop culture unfold before your eyes.

Cherry Blossom Season: Hanami and Sakura Viewing

The cherry blossom season in Japan, known as hanami, is a magical time of the year when the country's landscapes transform into a sea of delicate pink and white flowers. This chapter invites you to experience the enchantment of cherry blossoms, exploring the cultural significance, best viewing spots, and the joyous tradition of hanami.

The Symbolism of Cherry Blossoms:

Cherry blossoms, known as sakura in Japanese, hold deep symbolism in Japanese culture. They represent the transient nature of life, beauty, and renewal. The blossoms' ephemeral nature, blooming for only a short period before gently falling to the ground, serves as a reminder to cherish the present moment and embrace the beauty of life.

Timing and Forecast:

The cherry blossom season typically occurs in late March to early April, although the exact timing varies each year and depends on factors such as weather conditions and geographic location. The Japan Meteorological Corporation provides sakura forecasts, known as "sakura zensen," which predict the bloom dates across different regions of Japan. Checking these forecasts can help you plan your visit to coincide with the peak bloom.

Best Cherry Blossom Viewing Spots:

Japan boasts numerous picturesque locations for cherry blossom viewing, each offering a unique and breathtaking experience. Some of the most popular spots include Tokyo's Ueno Park, Kyoto's Maruyama Park, Osaka Castle Park, and the Philosopher's Path in Kyoto. These locations provide not only stunning vistas but also a festive atmosphere with food stalls, performances, and traditional hanami picnics.

Hanami Parties and Picnics:

Hanami is not just about admiring the cherry blossoms; it is also a time for celebration and gathering with friends, family, and colleagues. Many people participate in hanami parties, where they gather under the blooming trees, lay out picnic blankets, and enjoy food and drinks while reveling in the beauty of the blossoms. It is a joyous occasion filled with laughter, camaraderie, and appreciation for nature's splendor.

Nighttime Illuminations:

Some cherry blossom viewing spots offer nighttime illuminations, known as "yozakura," where the trees are lit up, creating a magical ambiance. These illuminations provide a different perspective, as the blossoms take on an ethereal glow against the dark sky. Parks, temples, and gardens often organize special events and extended hours during this time, allowing visitors to experience the enchantment of cherry blossoms after sunset.

Cherry Blossom Festivals:

Numerous festivals and events are held throughout Japan to celebrate the cherry blossom season. These festivals feature traditional performances, music, dance, and cultural activities. One of the most famous cherry blossom festivals is the Takayama Sakura Matsuri in Gifu Prefecture, where ornate festival floats adorned with cherry blossoms parade through the streets, creating a vibrant and festive atmosphere.

Beyond Honshu: Cherry Blossoms in Other Regions:

While Honshu, the main island of Japan, is renowned for its cherry blossoms, other regions also offer spectacular viewing opportunities. Hokkaido, the northernmost island, experiences a slightly later bloom, usually in late April to early May. The cherry blossoms in Hirosaki Park in Aomori Prefecture are particularly famous, and the Goryokaku Fort in Hakodate, Hokkaido, offers a unique cherry blossom viewing experience.

Hanami Etiquette:

Participating in hanami comes with certain etiquette to ensure a respectful and enjoyable experience for everyone. It is customary to avoid shaking the branches or picking the blossoms, as this may cause damage. Cleaning up after your hanami party and properly disposing of trash is also important. Additionally, showing consideration for others by not occupying a prime viewing spot for an extended period is appreciated.

Immersing yourself in the beauty of cherry

blossoms during hanami is an unforgettable experience that captures the essence of Japan's natural splendor and cultural heritage. Whether you choose to stroll through a park, join a hanami picnic, or attend a cherry blossom festival, the sight of the delicate petals fluttering in the breeze will leave you with a sense of awe and wonder. So, plan your visit accordingly, embrace the ephemeral beauty of sakura, and create cherished memories that will last a lifetime.

Festivals and Matsuri: Celebrating Japanese Traditions

Japan is a country steeped in rich cultural traditions, and one of the best ways to immerse yourself in its vibrant heritage is by participating in the lively festivals, known as matsuri. This chapter explores the diverse range of festivals held throughout the year, showcasing the captivating rituals, colorful parades, traditional performances, and joyful celebrations that make up Japan's festival calendar.

Matsuri: A Window into Japanese Culture:

Matsuri are traditional festivals deeply rooted in Japan's history and spiritual beliefs. They serve as a way to honor deities, give thanks for abundant harvests, commemorate historical events, and bring communities together. Matsuri are characterized by their vibrant displays of costumes, music, dance, processions, and delicious street food, creating a festive atmosphere that captivates both locals and visitors alike.

The Year-Round Festival Calendar:

Japan's festival calendar is filled with a wide array of events taking place throughout the year, each with its own unique theme, traditions, and regional variations. From the exuberant Sapporo Snow Festival in February to the dazzling Gion Matsuri in Kyoto in July, and the iconic Takayama Autumn Festival in October, there are countless opportunities to experience the vibrancy of Japanese festivals no matter the season.

Obon Festival: Honoring Ancestors:

One of the most significant and widely observed festivals in Japan is Obon, a time when ancestral spirits are believed to return to their families. Obon festivals typically involve bon dances, where participants dressed in yukata (summer kimono) circle around a central tower, dancing to traditional music. Lanterns are also lit to guide the spirits and create a serene atmosphere.

Tanabata Festival: Wishing upon the Stars:

Celebrated on the seventh day of the seventh month, the Tanabata Festival is inspired by a romantic legend of two celestial lovers who are only able to meet once a year. During this festival, colorful paper decorations and bamboo branches adorned with handwritten wishes are displayed, and various cultural performances and parades take place across the country.

Nebuta Festival: Exquisite Floats and Dynamic Parades:

The Nebuta Festival in Aomori Prefecture is known for its magnificent floats featuring large illuminated paper lanterns depicting mythical and historical figures. These floats are paraded through the streets, accompanied by taiko drumming, traditional music, and enthusiastic dancers wearing vibrant costumes. The Nebuta Festival is a visual spectacle that mesmerizes spectators with its grandeur.

Awa Odori: Dance to the Rhythm:

Awa Odori, held in Tokushima Prefecture, is

one of Japan's largest dance festivals. Thousands of participants, both professionals and amateurs, take to the streets, dancing to the beat of taiko drums and traditional folk music. The festival has a lively and energetic atmosphere, with spectators often joining in the procession, making it a truly inclusive celebration.

Kanamara Matsuri: Embracing Fertility:

Kanamara Matsuri, also known as the "Festival of the Steel Phallus," is a unique and cheeky festival held in Kawasaki. It celebrates fertility and promotes sexual health awareness. The highlight of the festival is a parade featuring large phallus-shaped decorations, humorous costumes, and a jovial atmosphere that embraces both tradition and modernity.

Matsuri Cuisine: Indulging in Festival Food:

No festival experience in Japan is complete without indulging in the delectable street food offerings. From savory delights like yakisoba (fried noodles) and takoyaki (octopus balls) to sweet treats like taiyaki (fish-shaped pastry) and shaved ice, festivals provide a gastronomic adventure for your taste buds. Each region boasts its own specialty dishes, ensuring a culinary journey to remember.

Hanagasa Matsuri: Dancing with Flower Hats:

The Hanagasa Matsuri in Yamagata Prefecture showcases a lively dance performed by participants wearing straw hats adorned with colorful paper flowers. The dance celebrates the beauty of summer and is accompanied by traditional music played on shamisen (a three-stringed instrument) and taiko drums. The Hanagasa Matsuri is a joyous event that exemplifies the harmony between nature and cultural expression.

Religious Festivals: Shrines and Temples:

Many matsuri have religious origins and are held at shrines or temples, combining spirituality with cultural festivities. These festivals often include rituals, processions of mikoshi (portable shrines), and ceremonial performances. Some notable religious festivals include the Sanja Matsuri in Tokyo's Asakusa district and the Kanda Matsuri held at Kanda Myojin Shrine, also in Tokyo.

Regional Festivals: Showcasing Local Traditions:

Each region of Japan has its own unique festivals that highlight local customs, folklore, and history. The Aomori Nebuta Festival, mentioned earlier, is just one example. Other regional festivals include the Hakata Gion Yamakasa in Fukuoka, the Yosakoi Festival in Kochi, and the Karatsu Kunchi Festival in Saga. Exploring these regional festivals offers insights into the distinct cultural identities of different areas in Japan.

Matsuri Attire and Accessories:

During matsuri, it is common for participants and attendees to dress in traditional attire such as yukata or happi coats. These garments add to the festive atmosphere and create a sense of unity among participants. Additionally, festival-goers often wear accessories like paper lanterns, festival masks, and colorful headbands, further enhancing the celebratory ambiance.

Attending a matsuri is an exhilarating and immersive experience that allows you to witness the vibrancy of Japanese traditions firsthand. Whether you find yourself surrounded by giant illuminated floats, dancing through the streets, or indulging in delicious festival food, the festivals of Japan offer a window into the country's cultural heritage and provide memories that will last a lifetime. So, embrace the spirit of celebration, join the locals in their festive revelry, and let the enchantment of matsuri transport you to the heart of Japanese culture.

Shrines and Temples: Spiritual Journeys in Japan

Japan is a country deeply rooted in spirituality, with a rich tapestry of shrines and temples that dot its landscapes. This chapter invites you on a spiritual journey, exploring the significance of these sacred sites, their architectural beauty, and the rituals and customs associated with them. Whether you seek tranquility, cultural exploration, or a deeper understanding of Japanese beliefs, visiting shrines and temples is an essential part of your journey through Japan.

The Sacredness of Shrines and Temples:

Shrines, known as "jinja," and temples, known as "tera" or "ji," hold great reverence in Japanese culture. Shrines are dedicated to Shintoism, the indigenous religion of Japan, which reveres various kami (deities) believed to reside in natural elements. Temples, on the other hand, are primarily associated with Buddhism, an influential religion in Japan. Both serve as places of worship, reflection, and connection with the divine.

Shinto Shrines: Connecting with Nature and Kami:

Shinto shrines are characterized by their simplicity, natural settings, and torii gates that mark the entrance to sacred grounds. They often have gardens, stone lanterns, and purification fountains, where visitors can cleanse themselves before entering. Popular shrines include Meiji Shrine in Tokyo, Fushimi Inari Taisha in Kyoto, and Itsukushima Shrine in Hiroshima, known for its iconic torii gate in the water.

Buddhist Temples: Serenity and Enlightenment:

Buddhist temples in Japan offer a serene atmosphere, intricate architecture, and opportunities for introspection. They house magnificent statues of Buddha, elaborate altars, and beautiful gardens. Notable temples include Kinkaku-ji (Golden Pavilion) in Kyoto, Todai-ji in Nara with its massive bronze Buddha, and Zen temples like Ryoan-ji and Daitoku-ji, where visitors can experience Zen meditation and tea ceremonies.

Purification and Rituals:

At both shrines and temples, purification rituals play an important role. Visitors may find ablution fountains where they can cleanse their hands and mouth before approaching the main hall or inner sanctuaries. It is customary to bow and offer a small donation at the altar, and at some temples, you can participate in chanting, praying, or even receive a blessing from a priest.

Omikuji and Ema: Seeking Guidance and Making Wishes:

Omikuji, or fortune-telling paper strips, are popular at both shrines and temples. Visitors can draw a strip that reveals their fortune or guidance for the future. Ema, wooden plaques, allow visitors to write their wishes and hang them on designated boards or trees. These customs provide a personal connection to the spiritual realm and allow for introspection and hope.

Pilgrimages: Following Sacred Paths:

Japan is famous for its spiritual pilgrimages, with some routes dating back centuries. The most renowned is the Shikoku Pilgrimage, which comprises 88 Buddhist temples associated with the monk Kukai, also known as Kobo Daishi. The Kumano Kodo in Wakayama Prefecture and the Nakasendo Trail connecting Kyoto and Tokyo are other notable pilgrimage routes that offer not only spiritual reflection but also breathtaking natural scenery.

Seasonal Festivals and Events:

Shrines and temples come alive during seasonal festivals and events, providing a unique opportunity to witness traditional rituals and cultural performances. Setsubun, the New Year's Eve festival, and the fire festivals of Nara and Kyoto are just a few examples. These celebrations offer a glimpse into the vibrant tapestry of Japanese traditions and beliefs.

Zen Buddhism: Mindfulness and Meditation:

For those seeking a deeper spiritual experience, Zen Buddhism offers practices of mindfulness and meditation. Zen temples provide meditation sessions called "zazen," where participants can learn to quiet the mind and find inner peace. Monastic stays, known as "shukubo," offer a chance to immerse yourself in the daily life of a temple and experience Zen teachings firsthand.

Gardens and Nature:

Many shrines and temples feature meticulously designed gardens that embody the principles of harmony, balance, and tranquility. These gardens, whether large or small, are meticulously maintained and offer a serene escape from the bustling world outside. The gardens often incorporate elements such as ponds, bridges, rock formations, and carefully pruned trees, inviting visitors to contemplate nature's beauty.

Spirituality in Modern Japan:

Shrines and temples continue to play a vital role in modern Japanese society. Despite technological advancements and societal changes, Japanese people often turn to these sacred places for solace, celebration, and connection to their cultural heritage. Witnessing the blend of ancient traditions and modern practices is a testament to the enduring power of spirituality in Japan.

Visiting shrines and temples in Japan is a gateway to the country's spiritual and cultural essence. Whether you are captivated by the tranquility of a Zen garden, seeking guidance through a fortune strip, or embracing the rituals of purification, these sacred sites provide a profound and immersive experience. So, embark on your spiritual journey, allow the hallowed atmosphere to envelop you, and discover the profound wisdom and beauty that lie within Japan's shrines and temples.

Traditional Arts and Crafts: Ikebana, Calligraphy, and Kimono

Japan is renowned for its rich artistic heritage, which encompasses a diverse range of traditional arts and crafts. From the delicate art of flower arrangement to the elegant strokes of calligraphy and the timeless beauty of kimono, these art forms provide a window into Japan's cultural identity and offer visitors a chance to immerse themselves in the country's artistic traditions. This chapter explores three iconic Japanese art forms: Ikebana, Calligraphy, and Kimono.

Ikebana: The Art of Flower Arrangement

Ikebana, also known as Kado or Kadō, is the Japanese art of flower arrangement. It goes beyond mere decoration and seeks to create a harmonious and contemplative expression of nature. Ikebana emphasizes simplicity, asymmetry, and the use of space. Each arrangement is carefully crafted, with attention given to the choice of flowers, their placement, and the vessel in which they are displayed. Ikebana schools such as Ikenobo, Ohara, and Sogetsu have their unique styles and approaches, showcasing the diversity of this art form.

Calligraphy: Expressing Beauty through Brush and Ink

Calligraphy, known as Shodo in Japanese, is the art of writing characters using a brush and ink. It is regarded as a highly disciplined and meditative practice that combines aesthetics with skillful technique. The beauty of calligraphy lies in the brushstrokes, which vary in thickness and rhythm, and the balance of the characters on the paper. Different scripts, such as kanji (Chinese characters), hiragana, and katakana, are used to write poetry, scriptures, and everyday expressions. Visitors can attend calligraphy classes, witness live demonstrations, or even try their hand at this elegant art form.

Kimono: The Timeless Japanese Garment

Kimono, the traditional Japanese garment, is an iconic symbol of Japanese culture. It is a T-shaped robe with straight-lined sleeves and a wraparound style, often made from silk or other exquisite fabrics. Kimono designs vary according to the occasion, season, and wearer's age or status. Each kimono is a work of art, featuring intricate patterns, vibrant colors, and meticulous craftsmanship. Visitors can learn about the different types of kimono, observe the process of kimono dressing, or even rent a kimono and experience the elegance firsthand.

Tea Ceremony: Harmony, Respect, and Tranquility

The Japanese tea ceremony, known as Chanoyu or Sado, is a cultural ritual that combines the preparation and serving of powdered green tea (matcha) with aesthetics, mindfulness, and social interaction. It is an art form that embodies principles such as harmony, respect, purity, and tranquility. The tea ceremony is conducted in a dedicated tea room, with guests following specific etiquette and procedures. Participating in a tea ceremony offers a unique glimpse into Japanese customs, aesthetics, and the profound philosophy of finding beauty in simplicity.

Traditional Crafts: Preserving Artistic Traditions

In addition to ikebana, calligraphy, and kimono, Japan is home to numerous traditional crafts that have been passed down through generations. These include pottery (such as Bizen, Arita, and Hagi ware), lacquerware, papermaking, woodworking, and textiles (such as silk weaving and dyeing techniques like Shibori and Yuzen). Many regions in Japan have their own specialty crafts, and visitors can explore craft centers, workshops, and museums to witness the mastery of these traditional techniques.

Engaging with traditional arts and crafts in Japan allows visitors to appreciate the meticulous attention to detail, the reverence for nature, and the profound cultural significance embedded within these art forms. Whether you attend an ikebana demonstration, learn the art of calligraphy, or experience the grace of wearing a kimono, these experiences offer a deeper understanding of Japan's artistic traditions and provide an opportunity for personal expression and connection with the country's cultural heritage. Immerse yourself in the world of ikebana, calligraphy, and kimono, and discover the enduring beauty and craftsmanship that define Japanese art.

Shopping in Japan: From Traditional Markets to High-End Fashion

Japan is a shopaholic's paradise, offering a diverse range of shopping experiences that cater to all tastes and budgets. From bustling traditional markets to luxurious high-end fashion districts, this chapter invites you to explore the vibrant world of shopping in Japan. Discover unique souvenirs, indulge in the latest fashion trends, and immerse yourself in the country's rich retail culture.

Traditional Markets: Exploring Local Treasures

Traditional markets, known as "shotengai" or "ichiba," are a window into Japan's culinary delights and local craftsmanship. These lively markets are bustling with activity and offer a wide array of fresh produce, traditional snacks, handmade crafts, and unique souvenirs. Some notable markets include Tsukiji Fish Market in Tokyo, Nishiki Market in Kyoto, and Kuromon Ichiba Market in Osaka. Stroll through the narrow streets, savor the aromas, and interact with local vendors to get a taste of authentic Japanese culture.

Department Stores: A Shopper's Haven

Japan is renowned for its department stores, which are not only shopping destinations but also cultural hubs. Major cities like Tokyo, Osaka, and Kyoto boast impressive department stores that cater to diverse interests. These multi-story retail complexes offer a wide range of goods, from high-end fashion brands to cosmetics, electronics, home goods, and gourmet food. Popular department stores include Mitsukoshi, Takashimaya, and Isetan, where you can enjoy a world-class shopping experience.

Fashion Districts: Setting Trends

Japan is a global fashion powerhouse, and its fashion districts are where trends are born. Harajuku in Tokyo is famous for its eclectic street fashion and unique boutiques, while Shibuya offers a mix of mainstream and cutting-edge fashion. In Osaka, the Minami district, particularly the Shinsaibashi and Amerikamura areas, is a fashion mecca. Explore these vibrant districts, discover avant-garde designs, and embrace the opportunity to update your wardrobe with stylish Japanese fashion.

Electronics and Gadgets: Embracing Technological Marvels

Japan is synonymous with cutting-edge technology, and its electronics stores are a testament to this. Akihabara in Tokyo is the epicenter of the country's electronics and otaku (geek) culture, offering an overwhelming selection of gadgets, anime merchandise, and video games. For a more sophisticated electronics shopping experience, visit large-scale retailers like Bic Camera and Yodobashi Camera, where you can find the latest gadgets, cameras, and home appliances.

Traditional Crafts and Souvenirs: Capturing the Essence of Japan

Japanese traditional crafts and souvenirs make for meaningful keepsakes and gifts. From delicate ceramics and lacquerware to exquisite textiles and traditional toys, there is something for everyone. Visit specialty stores and craft centers that showcase regional crafts, such as Kutani ceramics in Ishikawa Prefecture or Kokeshi dolls in Tohoku. Don't forget to explore the vibrant world of stationery, where you can find unique paper products, washi tape, and beautifully crafted writing tools.

Underground Shopping Arcades: Hidden Retail Gems

Japan's cities are crisscrossed with underground shopping arcades, known as "chika-gai" or "chika-town." These subterranean labyrinths are packed with shops, restaurants, and entertainment facilities, providing a convenient and sheltered shopping experience. From trendy boutiques to local eateries, these arcades offer a slice of Japanese urban life. Some notable examples include Sapporo's Tanuki Koji, Nagoya's Osu Shopping Street, and Tokyo's Ameya-Yokocho.

Outlet Malls: Bargain Hunting Extravaganza

For those seeking a shopping spree without breaking the bank, Japan's outlet malls are a treasure trove of discounted designer brands and affordable fashion. Outlet malls, such as Gotemba Premium Outlets near Mount Fuji, Mitsui Outlet Park near Osaka, and Rinku Premium Outlets near Kansai Airport, offer a wide range of international and Japanese brands at discounted prices. Enjoy significant savings while indulging in your favorite fashion labels.

Souvenir Food and Snacks: Tasting Japan's Flavors

No shopping experience in Japan is complete without exploring the realm of food souvenirs and snacks. From regional specialties to famous confectionery brands, there is an endless variety of treats to choose from. Sample traditional wagashi (Japanese sweets), indulge in matcha-flavored delights, and discover unique savory snacks like senbei (rice crackers) or regional delicacies. Don't forget to visit depachika (basement food halls) in department stores for a mouthwatering array of gourmet food options.

Shopping in Japan is more than just a commercial activity; it's an immersive cultural experience. Whether you're hunting for the latest fashion trends, seeking traditional crafts, or simply indulging in the vibrant atmosphere of local markets, the shopping scene in Japan offers a myriad of options to satisfy every shopper's desire. So, get ready to shop till you drop and uncover the hidden gems of retail therapy in this captivating country.

Japanese Gardens: Serenity and Harmony in Nature

Japanese gardens are enchanting spaces that showcase the beauty of nature and embody the principles of serenity and harmony. Designed with meticulous attention to detail, these gardens are serene havens that transport visitors to a world of tranquility and contemplation. This chapter explores the captivating allure of Japanese gardens and highlights some of the most renowned examples throughout the country.

The Essence of Japanese Gardens:

Japanese gardens are a reflection of the country's deep reverence for nature and its harmonious relationship with the environment. They seek to recreate the natural landscape in a controlled and refined manner, capturing the essence of mountains, rivers, and forests within a limited space. Every element in a Japanese garden, from rocks and water features to plants and ornaments, is carefully chosen and arranged to create a harmonious and balanced composition.

Garden Styles and Elements:

There are several distinct styles of Japanese gardens, each with its own characteristics and design principles. Some of the most notable styles include:

Karesansui (Dry Rock Gardens): These minimalist gardens feature carefully arranged rocks and raked gravel to evoke the essence of a landscape without the use of water.

Tsukiyama (Hill Gardens): These gardens recreate rolling hills and mountains, often incorporating ponds, bridges, and carefully placed vegetation to create a sense of depth and perspective.

Chaniwa (Tea Gardens): These gardens are specifically designed to enhance the tea ceremony experience, with features such as stone paths, tea houses, and serene contemplative spaces.

Stroll Gardens: These expansive gardens are designed for leisurely walks and contemplation. They often incorporate various elements, including ponds, bridges, pavilions, and meticulously pruned trees.

Zen Gardens: Finding Inner Peace:

Zen gardens, also known as "karesansui" or "dry rock gardens," hold a special place in Japanese garden design. These minimalist gardens, commonly found in Zen temples, feature carefully arranged rocks, raked gravel, and occasionally sparse vegetation. Zen gardens are intended to inspire contemplation and facilitate meditation, allowing visitors to find inner peace and tranquility in their serene simplicity.

Famous Japanese Gardens:

Japan is home to numerous world-renowned gardens, each offering a unique and unforgettable experience. Some of the most notable gardens include:

Ryoan-ji Temple Garden in Kyoto: This famous Zen garden is renowned for its arrangement of 15 rocks on a bed of raked white gravel. The simplicity and abstract nature of the design invite contemplation and introspection.

Kenrokuen Garden in Kanazawa: Considered one of Japan's most beautiful gardens, Kenrokuen features stunning landscapes, including ponds, bridges, teahouses, and meticulously pruned pine trees.

Katsura Imperial Villa in Kyoto: This historic villa boasts a breathtaking stroll garden with meticulously designed landscapes, including ponds, islands, stone lanterns, and teahouses. It exemplifies the elegance and sophistication of Japanese garden design.

Adachi Museum of Art Garden in Shimane: This garden is known for its seamless integration of art and nature. The meticulously maintained landscape serves as a living canvas, beautifully complementing the museum's collection of Japanese paintings.

The Four Elements of Japanese Gardens:

Japanese gardens often incorporate the four essential elements: rocks, water, plants, and ornaments. These elements are carefully arranged to create a balanced and harmonious composition. Rocks represent the enduring and unchanging aspect of nature, while water symbolizes life and movement. Plants, including trees, shrubs, and flowers, provide seasonal beauty and contribute to the overall ambiance. Ornamental elements such as stone lanterns, bridges, and pagodas add cultural and symbolic significance to the garden.

Visiting a Japanese garden is an opportunity to immerse oneself in the serene beauty of nature and experience the principles of harmony and balance deeply ingrained in Japanese culture. Whether strolling through a traditional tea garden, contemplating the simplicity of a Zen garden, or marveling at the artistry of a meticulously designed landscape, these gardens offer a respite from the bustling modern world, inviting visitors to connect with the tranquility and serenity that lie within.

Mountaineering and Hiking: Conquering Japan's Peaks

Japan's rugged terrain, with its majestic peaks and breathtaking landscapes, offers an exhilarating playground for mountaineering and hiking enthusiasts. From iconic mountains like Mount Fuji to hidden gems in remote regions, this chapter explores the allure of mountaineering and hiking in Japan, providing essential information and tips for adventurers seeking to conquer the country's peaks.

Mount Fuji: A Symbol of Japan

No discussion of mountaineering in Japan would be complete without mentioning Mount Fuji. As the highest peak in the country and a UNESCO World Heritage site, Mount Fuji attracts climbers from around the world. Scaling its iconic cone-shaped summit is a popular challenge during the climbing season, which typically runs from July to September. Be prepared for a demanding ascent, but the reward is an awe-inspiring sunrise from the summit and panoramic views of the surrounding landscape.

Japan's Mountain Ranges:

Japan is blessed with several mountain ranges that offer a wide range of hiking and mountaineering opportunities. The Japan Alps, including the Northern, Central, and Southern Alps, are famous for their towering peaks and alpine landscapes. The Dewa Sanzan in Tohoku and the Tateyama Kurobe Alpine Route in the

Chubu region are other popular destinations for mountain enthusiasts. Each range presents its own unique challenges and rewards, making them a paradise for outdoor adventurers.

Essential Equipment and Safety Precautions:

Proper equipment and safety precautions are vital when embarking on a mountaineering or hiking expedition in Japan. Here are some key considerations:

Clothing and Footwear: Dress in layers to adapt to changing weather conditions, and wear sturdy hiking boots that provide ankle support and good traction.

Navigation and Communication: Carry a detailed topographic map, a compass or GPS device, and a fully charged mobile phone for navigation and emergency purposes.

Weather Awareness: Check the weather forecast before setting out, and be prepared for sudden changes in weather conditions, particularly in higher altitudes.

Hydration and Nutrition: Carry enough water and snacks to stay hydrated and energized throughout your journey. Refill stations are available at some mountain huts, but it's always advisable to carry extra supplies.

Mountaineering Insurance: Consider purchasing mountaineering insurance that covers emergency evacuation and medical expenses in case of accidents or unforeseen circumstances.

Hiking Trails and Routes:

Japan boasts a vast network of hiking trails that cater to all skill levels, from leisurely day hikes to challenging multi-day treks. Some popular routes include:

Kumano Kodo: A network of ancient pilgrimage trails in the Kii Peninsula, offering a chance to immerse yourself in Japan's spiritual and natural heritage.

Nakasendo Trail: An ancient route connecting Kyoto and Tokyo, dotted with historical towns, scenic landscapes, and charming rural villages.

Yakushima Island: Known for its ancient cedar forests and diverse flora and fauna, Yakushima offers a range of hiking trails suitable for different levels of experience.

Oze National Park: A vast marshland in Gunma and Niigata Prefectures, with a network of boardwalks and trails that allow visitors to explore its unique alpine flora and fauna.

Seasonal Considerations:

Japan experiences distinct seasons, and the best time for mountaineering and hiking varies depending on the region and elevation. Consider the following:

Spring: Spring is an ideal time for lower elevation hikes when cherry blossoms and other flowers are in bloom. It's also a popular season for traversing the Japanese Alps.

Summer: Summer is the main climbing season for Mount Fuji and high-altitude hikes. Be prepared for crowded trails and check weather conditions, as storms can be a concern.

Autumn: Autumn brings vibrant foliage, making it a picturesque time for hiking in mountainous areas such as the Japan Alps and Nikko.

Winter: Winter hiking is possible in some regions, but it requires experience, appropriate gear, and caution due to snow and icy conditions.

Etiquette and Respect for Nature:

When exploring Japan's mountains, it's essential to adhere to the principles of Leave No Trace and show respect for the environment and local customs. Remember to:

Pack out all waste and litter, leaving the trails and campsites pristine.

Observe any trail restrictions or closures, especially in protected areas or during wildlife breeding seasons.

Be mindful of noise levels, especially when hiking near residential areas or sacred sites.

Show respect for local culture and customs, including following any specific guidelines for visiting temples, shrines, or sacred mountains.

Embarking on a mountaineering or hiking adventure in Japan is a rewarding experience that allows you to connect with the country's stunning natural beauty and challenge your physical and mental limits. Whether you aim to conquer iconic peaks, explore hidden valleys, or simply enjoy the serenity of nature, Japan's mountains offer a wealth of opportunities for outdoor enthusiasts and a chance to create unforgettable memories.

Rural Japan: Exploring Traditional Villages and Countryside

While Japan is often associated with its bustling cities and modern advancements, the country's rural areas offer a glimpse into its rich cultural heritage and picturesque landscapes. This chapter delves into the charm of rural Japan, highlighting traditional villages and the beauty of the countryside, where time seems to stand still.

Embracing the Slow Pace of Life:

In rural Japan, life moves at a more relaxed pace, providing an escape from the fast-paced city environment. Visitors can immerse themselves in the tranquility of the countryside, where nature's rhythms and the simplicity of everyday life take center stage. It's an opportunity to slow down, savor the moment, and appreciate the beauty of the simpler things in life.

Traditional Villages:

Rural Japan is home to numerous traditional villages that have preserved their cultural heritage over centuries. These villages showcase traditional architecture, local customs, and a way of life deeply rooted in tradition. Some noteworthy villages to explore include:

Shirakawa-go and Gokayama: Located in the mountainous region of Gifu and Toyama Prefectures, these UNESCO World Heritage sites are renowned for their picturesque thatched-roof houses, known as gassho-zukuri, which are architectural marvels designed to withstand heavy snowfall.

Ouchi-juku: Nestled in the mountains of Fukushima Prefecture, Ouchi-juku offers a glimpse into the Edo period with its well-preserved thatched-roof houses and a tranquil atmosphere reminiscent of the olden days.

Miyama: Situated in Kyoto Prefecture, Miyama is known for its charming thatched-roof houses and serene countryside. The village provides an idyllic setting for leisurely strolls and experiencing rural Japanese life.

Farming Traditions and Agriculture:

Agriculture has played a crucial role in Japan's history and continues to be a vital part of rural life. Many regions offer opportunities to experience agricultural traditions firsthand, from participating in rice planting and harvesting to learning traditional farming techniques. Visitors can also savor farm-to-table experiences by indulging in fresh, locally grown produce and regional specialties.

Onsen Retreats in Rural Settings:

Rural Japan is dotted with onsen, natural hot springs that offer relaxation and rejuvenation for both locals and travelers. These hot springs often provide a serene escape amidst scenic landscapes, allowing visitors to soak in mineral-rich waters while surrounded by nature's beauty. Some rural onsen towns worth exploring include Kinosaki Onsen in Hyogo Prefecture and Yufuin in Oita Prefecture.

Exploring Nature's Beauty:

The countryside of Japan boasts breathtaking landscapes that vary with the seasons. From vibrant cherry blossoms in spring to colorful foliage in autumn, the changing scenery paints a picturesque backdrop for outdoor activities such as hiking, cycling, and nature walks. National parks like Nikko, Aso, and Shiretoko offer opportunities to explore diverse ecosystems and encounter unique wildlife.

Cultural Festivals and Traditions:

Rural Japan is known for its vibrant festivals and cultural traditions, which are deeply ingrained in local communities. These festivals celebrate everything from bountiful harvests to ancient rituals and provide an opportunity for visitors to witness traditional music, dance, and folklore. The Takayama Festival in Gifu Prefecture and Nebuta Festival in Aomori Prefecture are just a couple of examples of the cultural vibrancy that can be experienced in rural areas.

Homestays and Local Hospitality:

One of the best ways to immerse oneself in rural Japan is through homestays or farm stays. These experiences allow visitors to interact with locals, gain insights into their way of life, and forge meaningful connections. Homestays often include home-cooked meals made with locally sourced ingredients, providing a taste of authentic Japanese cuisine and hospitality.

Visiting rural Japan offers a unique perspective

on the country's culture, traditions, and natural beauty. Whether exploring traditional villages, engaging in agricultural activities, or simply taking in the serene countryside, this chapter encourages travelers to step off the beaten path and discover the hidden gems that rural Japan has to offer. It's a chance to reconnect with nature, experience the warmth of local communities, and create lasting memories of a Japan beyond the cityscapes.

Transportation in Japan: Navigating the Efficient Rail Network

When it comes to getting around Japan, the country's efficient and extensive rail network is a traveler's best friend. Renowned for its punctuality, comfort, and convenience, the rail system in Japan offers an unparalleled experience for exploring the country. This chapter will guide you through the ins and outs of navigating Japan's rail network, ensuring a smooth and seamless journey.

Japan Rail Pass:

The Japan Rail Pass is a cost-effective and convenient option for travelers planning to explore multiple regions in Japan. This pass allows unlimited travel on most Japan Railways (JR) trains, including the famous shinkansen (bullet trains), for a fixed duration of time. It is available in different durations (7, 14, or 21 days) and can be purchased in advance from authorized vendors outside of Japan.

Shinkansen: High-Speed Rail Travel:

The shinkansen is an iconic symbol of Japan's transportation prowess. These high-speed trains connect major cities across the country, offering swift and comfortable travel. With speeds reaching up to 320 km/h (200 mph), the shinkansen allows travelers to reach their destinations quickly and efficiently. Each train is equipped with comfortable seating, ample legroom, and onboard amenities, making the journey a pleasurable experience.

Regional and Local Trains:

In addition to the shinkansen, Japan's rail network includes a comprehensive system of regional and local trains. These trains connect smaller towns, scenic areas, and off-the-beaten-path destinations. While they may not be as fast as the shinkansen, regional and local trains offer a chance to experience the local culture and scenery at a more relaxed pace.

IC Cards:

IC cards, such as Suica, Pasmo, and ICOCA, are rechargeable smart cards that provide a convenient and cashless way to pay for train fares, as well as other forms of transportation and purchases at select retailers. These cards can be easily obtained and recharged at train stations, and they offer the flexibility to travel seamlessly across different rail networks without the need for purchasing individual tickets.

Hyperdia and Rail Apps:

Hyperdia is a popular online timetable and route planner for train travel in Japan. It allows users to search for the most efficient routes, check train schedules, and calculate fares. Additionally, various rail apps, such as Japan Official Travel App and Navitime, provide real-time information, platform guidance, and other useful features to assist travelers in navigating the rail system.

Seat Reservations:

For longer journeys or peak travel periods, it is advisable to make seat reservations, especially on shinkansen trains. Seat reservations can be made at ticket offices or using ticket machines at train stations. This ensures a guaranteed seat and allows travelers to relax and enjoy the journey without the worry of finding available seating.

Baggage Handling and Lockers:

Many train stations in Japan offer baggage handling services and coin-operated lockers for travelers to store their luggage. These services are particularly useful if you are traveling with bulky or heavy bags and want to explore a city or visit attractions without being burdened by your belongings.

Etiquette on Trains:

When traveling on trains in Japan, it's important to observe certain etiquette to ensure a pleasant experience for everyone. These etiquettes include:

Standing on the correct side of escalators to allow others to pass.

Offering seats to those in need, such as the elderly, pregnant women, or people with disabilities.

Keeping noise levels low and refraining from talking loudly on the phone.

Avoiding eating or drinking in crowded trains, as it is generally discouraged.

Rail Passes for Local Areas:

In addition to the Japan Rail Pass, some regions offer local rail passes that cater specifically to tourists exploring specific areas. These passes provide unlimited travel on local trains, buses, and ferries within a designated region for a set period. They can be a cost-effective option for those planning to stay in a particular region and explore its attractions extensively.

Other Modes of Transportation:

While the rail network is the backbone of transportation in Japan, other modes of transportation can complement your travel experience. This includes buses, trams, ferries, and even domestic flights for longer distances or remote islands. It's worth considering these options, depending on your itinerary and desired destinations.

Navigating Japan's rail network is an adventure in itself. With its efficiency, reliability, and coverage, the rail system provides a seamless means of transportation for travelers exploring the country. By familiarizing yourself with the Japan Rail Pass, understanding the different types of trains, and utilizing smart cards and route-planning apps, you can make the most of your journey and experience the convenience of Japan's world-class rail network.

Japanese Language Survival Guide: Basic Phrases and Tips

While traveling in Japan, knowing a few basic Japanese phrases can go a long way in enhancing your experience and connecting with the locals. This chapter serves as a Japanese language survival guide, equipping you with essential phrases and cultural tips to navigate common situations and interact with confidence.

Greetings and Introductions:

Mastering basic greetings is key to starting any conversation. Learn phrases like "Konnichiwa" (Hello), "Arigatou gozaimasu" (Thank you), and "Sumimasen" (Excuse me) to express politeness and respect. When meeting someone for the first time, a simple "Hajimemashite" (Nice to meet you) will suffice.

Asking for Help and Directions:

When in need of assistance or directions, it's helpful to know phrases like "Eigo o hanasemasu ka?" (Do you speak English?), "Doko desu ka?" (Where is it?), and "Onegaishimasu, _____ o misete kudasai" (Please show me _____). Locals appreciate your efforts to communicate in their language, even if your proficiency is limited.

Ordering Food and Drinks:

Exploring Japan's culinary delights is a must, and being able to order food and drinks in Japanese adds to the experience. Familiarize yourself with phrases such as "O-negai shimasu" (Please), "Kore o kudasai" (I'll have this), and "Osusume wa nan desu ka?" (What do you recommend?). Don't forget to say "Gochisousama deshita" (Thank you for the meal) at the end of your dining experience.

Shopping and Bargaining:

When shopping in Japan, a few useful phrases can help you navigate stores and markets. Use phrases like "Ikura desu ka?" (How much is it?), "Chotto takai desu" (It's a bit expensive), and "Gimme ga arimasu ka?" (Do you have a discount?). Politeness and respectful gestures are valued during transactions.

Cultural Etiquette:

Understanding and respecting Japanese cultural norms can enhance your interactions with locals. For example, saying "O-jama shimasu" (Excuse me for intruding) when entering someone's home or "O-tsukare-sama desu" (You must be tired) to acknowledge someone's hard work or effort are considered polite gestures. Additionally, learning to bow slightly when greeting or thanking someone shows respect.

Emergency Situations:

While nobody hopes for emergencies, it's essential to be prepared. Familiarize yourself with phrases like "Tasukete kudasai" (Please help me), "Kyuukyuu sha o yonde kudasai" (Please call an ambulance), and "Keisatsu o yonde kudasai" (Please call the police) in case of urgent situations.

Using Language Apps and Phrasebooks:

To supplement your language learning, consider using language apps like Duolingo or

Memrise, or carry a pocket-sized phrasebook. These resources can provide additional phrases, pronunciation guides, and useful vocabulary to enhance your communication skills.

Learning Basic Kanji and Kana:

Although learning the entire Japanese writing system may be challenging, familiarizing yourself with basic kanji (Chinese characters) and kana (hiragana and katakana) can be advantageous. Recognizing common signs, reading menus, and understanding basic instructions become easier with this knowledge.

Embracing Mistakes and Having Fun:

Learning a new language is an ongoing process, and making mistakes is part of the journey. Embrace the opportunity to learn and grow, and don't be afraid to laugh at yourself. The locals appreciate your efforts, and even simple attempts at using Japanese can open doors to memorable interactions.

Seeking Language Assistance:

If you find yourself struggling to communicate or comprehend, don't hesitate to seek language assistance. Many Japanese people are willing to help, and language barriers can often be overcome through gestures, visuals, or the use of translation apps.

By arming yourself with these basic phrases and tips, you'll navigate Japan with greater ease and foster meaningful connections with locals. Remember, learning a few words in the local language shows respect and can lead to unforgettable experiences during your travels in Japan.

Money Matters: Currency, Budgeting, and Tipping

Understanding the currency, managing your budget, and knowing the tipping customs are crucial aspects of your travel experience in Japan. This chapter will guide you through the essentials of handling money, ensuring a smooth financial journey during your time in the country.

Currency in Japan:

The official currency of Japan is the Japanese yen (JPY). Familiarize yourself with the denominations, including coins (1, 5, 10, 50, 100, and 500 yen) and banknotes (1,000, 2,000, 5,000, and 10,000 yen). It's advisable to carry a mix of cash and cards, as some establishments, especially in rural areas, may not accept credit or debit cards.

Exchange Rates and Currency Exchange:

Before your trip, keep an eye on exchange rates to get an idea of how much your home currency is worth in yen. Currency exchange can be done at airports, banks, post offices, or dedicated currency exchange counters in major cities. ATMs in Japan also allow cash withdrawals using international debit or credit cards, but check with your bank regarding fees and foreign transaction charges.

Budgeting for Your Trip:

To ensure a smooth financial journey, it's important to establish a budget for your trip to Japan. Research the average costs of accommodation, transportation, meals, attractions, and souvenirs in the cities or regions you plan to visit. Consider any additional expenses such as travel insurance, transportation passes, or special activities you wish to partake in. This will help you estimate your daily expenditure and plan accordingly.

Cash-Based Society:

While Japan is a technologically advanced country, it remains predominantly cash-based, especially in smaller establishments, traditional markets, and local eateries. It's recommended to carry sufficient cash for day-to-day expenses. ATMs are widely available, but ensure you withdraw money during business hours as some ATMs may be inaccessible during evenings or weekends.

Credit and Debit Cards:

Credit and debit cards are accepted in major hotels, department stores, large restaurants, and tourist-oriented businesses. However, it's always a good idea to carry some cash as backup, especially in rural areas or when visiting smaller establishments. Notify your bank or card provider about your travel plans to avoid any potential card usage issues.

Tipping Culture:

Tipping is not customary in Japan and is often considered unnecessary. In fact, attempting to tip may cause confusion or be politely refused. Service charges are typically included in the bill at hotels and high-end restaurants. Instead of tipping, show appreciation by saying "Gochisousama deshita" (Thank you for the meal) or expressing gratitude with a polite bow.

Tax-Free Shopping:

Foreign tourists visiting Japan are eligible for tax-free shopping under certain conditions. Look for stores displaying the "Tax-Free" logo and be prepared to present your passport at the time of purchase. Keep in mind that not all items are eligible for tax exemption, and there may be minimum spending requirements. You can claim the tax refund at designated counters at the airport before departure.

Money-Saving Tips:

To make the most of your budget, consider these money-saving tips:

Utilize discount passes for transportation, such as the Japan Rail Pass or regional passes, if they align with your itinerary.

Explore affordable dining options, such as local eateries, food stalls, or convenience stores, which offer delicious and inexpensive meals.

Visit free or low-cost attractions, parks, and gardens, which allow you to experience the beauty and culture of Japan without breaking the bank.

Take advantage of happy hour specials or lunchtime discounts at restaurants for affordable dining experiences.

Shop at local markets or tax-free shops for unique souvenirs at reasonable prices.

Consider staying in budget accommodations like guesthouses, hostels, or capsule hotels, which offer affordable options without compromising comfort.

By familiarizing yourself with the currency, managing your budget effectively, and understanding the tipping customs in Japan, you can navigate the financial aspects of your trip with confidence. Remember to plan ahead, carry sufficient cash, and embrace the cash-based culture of the country. With careful budgeting and money-saving strategies, you can fully enjoy your time in Japan without worrying about financial constraints.

Safety and Health: Staying Secure and Healthy in Japan

When traveling to Japan, it's important to prioritize your safety and well-being. This chapter provides essential information and tips to ensure a secure and healthy journey throughout your time in the country.

General Safety Precautions:

Japan is known for its overall safety, but it's still important to exercise caution and be mindful of your surroundings. Keep these general safety precautions in mind:

Carry a copy of your passport and important documents, and leave the originals in a secure place.

Be aware of your belongings at all times, especially in crowded areas. Avoid displaying valuable items or carrying large sums of cash.

Use lockers provided at train stations or accommodation to store your luggage securely when exploring.

Follow traffic rules and be cautious when crossing the road. Remember that traffic in Japan drives on the left side.

Familiarize yourself with emergency contact numbers, including the police (110) and ambulance/medical services (119).

Health and Medical Care:

Japan boasts a high standard of healthcare facilities and services. To ensure your well-being during your trip:

Consider purchasing travel insurance that covers medical expenses, trip cancellation, and emergency evacuation.

Pack a basic first aid kit with essential items such as band-aids, pain relievers, antiseptic wipes, and any necessary prescription medications.

Familiarize yourself with the location of hospitals, clinics, and pharmacies in the areas you plan to visit. English-speaking medical facilities can be found in major cities and tourist destinations.

Check if you require any vaccinations before traveling to Japan and consult with your healthcare provider well in advance.

Practice good hygiene, such as washing your hands regularly and carrying hand sanitizer for times when soap and water are not readily available.

Natural Disasters:

Japan is prone to natural disasters, including earthquakes, typhoons, and tsunamis. While the likelihood of encountering such events during your trip is low, it's essential to be prepared:

Stay informed about local weather conditions and any potential warnings or advisories issued by local authorities.

Follow instructions from hotel staff or local authorities in the event of an earthquake or natural disaster. Familiarize yourself with emergency evacuation routes and designated shelters.

Register your travel plans with your embassy

or consulate, so they can provide assistance and updates if needed.

Carry a small emergency kit with essentials like a flashlight, portable phone charger, whistle, and non-perishable food items.

Food and Water Safety:

Japan is known for its delicious cuisine, but it's important to prioritize food and water safety to avoid any health issues:

Tap water is generally safe to drink throughout Japan, but if you prefer bottled water, it is widely available for purchase.

When dining at restaurants, choose establishments with good hygiene practices and a steady flow of customers.

Be cautious when consuming raw or undercooked seafood or meats. If you have dietary restrictions or allergies, communicate your needs clearly to restaurant staff.

Wash fruits and vegetables thoroughly or opt for peeled and cooked options when unsure about their source or quality.

Traveling Alone and Personal Safety:

Japan is considered a safe destination for solo travelers, but it's still important to prioritize personal safety:

Share your itinerary and contact information with a trusted friend or family member.

Avoid walking alone in unlit or isolated areas, especially at night. Stick to well-populated and well-lit areas.

Use reputable transportation options, especially when traveling late at night.

Trust your instincts and be cautious when interacting with strangers. If you feel uncomfortable or unsafe, remove yourself from the situation.

Respect local customs and cultural norms to avoid any misunderstandings or unintentional offense.

By following these safety and health tips, you can ensure a secure and worry-free journey in Japan. Stay informed, prioritize your well-being, and embrace the peace of mind that comes with exploring this captivating country.

Solo Travel in Japan: Tips for Independent Explorers

Traveling solo in Japan offers a unique and rewarding experience, allowing you the freedom to immerse yourself in the rich culture, explore hidden gems, and create unforgettable memories. This chapter provides valuable tips and insights to make the most of your solo adventure in Japan.

Embrace the Safety:

One of the greatest advantages of traveling solo in Japan is the country's reputation for safety. Japan consistently ranks as one of the safest countries in the world, with low crime rates and a reliable public transportation system. Embrace this sense of security but remain vigilant and take necessary precautions to ensure your personal safety.

Plan and Research:

As a solo traveler, thorough planning and research are key to a successful trip. Before your journey, familiarize yourself with the destinations you plan to visit, including their attractions, transportation options, and local customs. Create an itinerary that aligns with your interests but also allows for flexibility to embrace unexpected discoveries.

Accommodation Choices:

When choosing accommodations as a solo traveler, consider the type of experience you're seeking. Hostels and guesthouses provide opportunities to meet fellow travelers, while hotels offer privacy and comfort. Consider staying in centrally located accommodations with easy access to transportation, amenities, and attractions.

Engage with Locals:

Interacting with locals can enrich your solo travel experience in Japan. While language barriers may exist, don't be afraid to engage in simple conversations, seek recommendations, or ask for directions. Japanese people are generally friendly and helpful, and even a basic greeting or a smile can go a long way in forging connections.

Transportation Convenience:

Japan's efficient and extensive transportation network makes it convenient for solo travelers to navigate the country. Take advantage of the Shinkansen (bullet train) for long-distance travel, regional passes for cost-effective transportation, and local trains and buses for exploring within cities and towns. Use mobile apps or websites to plan your routes and check schedules.

Dining Alone:

Eating alone in Japan is a common practice, and there are numerous options available for solo diners. Embrace the local food culture by trying a variety of Japanese cuisine, from street food to traditional restaurants. Many eateries offer counter seating, where you can observe the chefs at work and engage in casual conversations with fellow diners.

Enjoying Solo Activities:

Japan offers a plethora of activities suitable for

solo travelers. Take the opportunity to immerse yourself in traditional Japanese arts, such as tea ceremonies, calligraphy, or ikebana (flower arrangement). Explore museums, gardens, and temples at your own pace, savor the tranquility of a hot spring (onsen), or indulge in a relaxing solo hike in nature.

Photography and Capturing Memories:

As a solo traveler, you have the freedom to capture the beauty of Japan through your lens. Whether you're an amateur or a photography enthusiast, take advantage of the stunning landscapes, vibrant cityscapes, and cultural moments to document your journey. Remember to be respectful when taking photos, especially in sacred or private spaces.

Stay Connected:

Maintaining connectivity while traveling solo in Japan is essential for convenience and safety. Consider obtaining a pocket Wi-Fi device or purchasing a local SIM card to stay connected to the internet, access maps, translation apps, and communicate with family and friends. Share your experiences through social media and connect with fellow travelers.

Self-Reflection and Self-Care:

Solo travel provides a unique opportunity for self-reflection and self-care. Take time to recharge and indulge in activities that bring you joy and relaxation. Engage in meditation, yoga, or simply enjoy a peaceful moment in a serene garden.

Reflect on your experiences, embrace the solitude, and appreciate the personal growth that comes with traveling alone.

Traveling solo in Japan is an empowering and transformative experience. Embrace the freedom, immerse yourself in the rich culture, and allow the country's enchanting landscapes and warm hospitality to create lifelong memories. With careful planning, an open mind, and a spirit of adventure, you'll discover the magic of Japan and yourself along the way.

Family-Friendly Japan: Activities for Kids and Parents

Traveling to Japan with your family provides a wonderful opportunity to create lasting memories and introduce your children to a rich cultural experience. From captivating attractions to engaging activities, Japan offers a wide range of family-friendly options. This chapter will guide you through some of the best activities and destinations that will delight both kids and parents alike.

Theme Parks and Amusement Parks:

Japan is home to a variety of world-class theme parks that cater to all ages. Some of the most popular choices include:

Tokyo Disneyland and Tokyo DisneySea: Experience the magic of Disney in Tokyo with thrilling rides, parades, and beloved characters.

Universal Studios Japan (Osaka): Step into the world of movies with exciting rides and attractions based on blockbuster films.

Fuji-Q Highland (Fujiyoshida): Enjoy adrenaline-pumping roller coasters and breathtaking views of Mount Fuji.

Legoland Japan (Nagoya): Let your children's creativity soar with Lego-themed rides, play areas, and building experiences.

Interactive Museums and Science Centers:

Japan boasts several interactive museums and science centers that make learning fun for the whole family. Consider these engaging options:

National Museum of Emerging Science and Innovation (Miraikan, Tokyo): Explore cutting-edge science and technology exhibits, including interactive displays and robots.

Kyoto Railway Museum: Delve into the fascinating world of trains with hands-on exhibits, train simulators, and even the opportunity to operate miniature railways.

Odaiba Palette Town (Tokyo): Visit the MEGA WEB theme park, where children can test drive electric cars and try their hand at virtual reality experiences.

Children's Museum (Saitama): Engage in interactive exhibits focused on science, nature, and creativity, allowing kids to learn through play.

Animal Encounters and Aquariums:

Children are often fascinated by animals, and Japan offers numerous opportunities for up-close encounters:

Ueno Zoo (Tokyo): Explore one of Japan's oldest and most renowned zoos, home to a diverse range of animals, including giant pandas.

Nara Park (Nara): Interact with friendly deer, considered sacred in Japanese culture, and enjoy the picturesque surroundings.

Okinawa Churaumi Aquarium (Okinawa): Marvel at the impressive marine life, including whale sharks, manta rays, and colorful tropical fish.

Asahiyama Zoo (Hokkaido): Witness unique animal exhibits, such as penguins walking freely and polar bears swimming underwater.

Traditional Cultural Experiences:

Immerse your family in the rich traditions and cultural heritage of Japan:

Samurai and Ninja Experiences (Kyoto and Tokyo): Dress up in traditional samurai or ninja attire, learn about their history, and participate in sword-fighting or shuriken-throwing activities.

Kimono Dressing and Tea Ceremony: Experience the elegance of Japan's traditional clothing by dressing in a kimono and partake in a tea ceremony, learning the art of tea preparation and etiquette.

Manga and Anime Tours (Tokyo): Visit themed cafes, anime merchandise stores, and attend cosplay events to explore the vibrant world of Japanese pop culture.

Kabuki or Noh Theater Performances: Witness captivating performances of classical Japanese theater, featuring elaborate costumes, music, and dance.

Parks and Gardens:

Japan is known for its beautifully manicured parks and gardens, offering tranquil spaces for relaxation and play:

Shinjuku Gyoen National Garden (Tokyo): Enjoy expansive lawns, cherry blossom trees, and peaceful walking paths.

Hiroshima Peace Memorial Park (Hiroshima): Learn about history while strolling through this peaceful park, dedicated to promoting peace and understanding.

Yoyogi Park (Tokyo): Explore this vast park, known for its vibrant atmosphere, street performers, and open spaces for picnics and games.

Arashiyama Bamboo Grove (Kyoto): Walk through the enchanting bamboo forest and visit the nearby Monkey Park for a unique experience.

Family-friendly Food Adventures:

Introduce your children to the delights of Japanese cuisine through interactive and kid-friendly dining experiences:

Conveyor Belt Sushi Restaurants: Let your children choose their favorite sushi dishes from a rotating conveyor belt, making mealtime interactive and fun.

Food-themed Theme Parks: Visit places like Pallet Town (Yokohama) or Ramen Street (Tokyo Station) to indulge in a variety of culinary delights.

Cooking Classes: Enroll in a family-friendly cooking class where you can learn to make sushi, bento boxes, or traditional Japanese sweets together.

Character Cafes: Treat your children to a unique dining experience at one of Japan's character-themed cafes, featuring beloved animated characters.

Japan offers endless possibilities for family-friendly adventures, blending education, entertainment, and cultural immersion. Embrace the opportunities to create cherished memories as you explore the wonders of Japan with your loved ones. Remember to plan ahead, check for age restrictions, and enjoy the journey together.

Accessibility in Japan: Traveling with Disabilities

Japan is a country known for its rich cultural heritage, stunning landscapes, and warm hospitality. For travelers with disabilities, exploring Japan may seem like a daunting task. However, Japan has made significant efforts to improve accessibility and create an inclusive environment for all visitors. This chapter aims to provide useful information and tips for travelers with disabilities, ensuring that they can enjoy a fulfilling and comfortable experience in Japan.

Infrastructure and Facilities:

Japan has implemented various measures to improve accessibility in public spaces and transportation systems. Here are some key considerations:

Accessible Transportation: Many train stations and buses in major cities are equipped with elevators, ramps, and priority seating for individuals with disabilities. Additionally, major airports provide wheelchair-accessible facilities and support services.

Barrier-Free Accommodations: Numerous hotels in Japan offer barrier-free rooms with accessible features such as widened doorways, grab bars, and roll-in showers. It is advisable to book accommodations in advance and inform them of any specific accessibility requirements.

Public Restrooms: Look for restrooms marked with the International Symbol of Access (ISA) or the "Toilet" symbol. Some restrooms are equipped with spacious stalls, grab bars, and other accessibility features.

Sidewalks and Crosswalks: Many urban areas have wide and well-maintained sidewalks with tactile paving to assist individuals with visual impairments. Crosswalks often have audible signals or tactile indicators to aid pedestrians.

Assistance and Support:

Traveling with a disability may require additional support. Japan offers several resources to ensure a smooth and enjoyable trip:

Tourist Information Centers: Visit tourist information centers in major cities, where staff members can provide guidance, maps, and information on accessible attractions and facilities.

Japan Accessible Tourism Center (JATC): JATC offers comprehensive information on accessible accommodations, transportation, and attractions in multiple languages. Their website and helpline can be valuable resources for planning your trip.

Personal Support Services: Some tour companies and organizations offer guided tours and personal support services specifically tailored to the needs of travelers with disabilities. These services can assist with transportation, communication, and accessing attractions.

Disability Identification Cards: If you have a disability, consider obtaining an International Disability Identification Card or a relevant document in your home country. While not required, it can help communicate your needs and access certain benefits or services.

Accessible Attractions and Experiences:

Japan offers a diverse range of accessible attractions that showcase its culture and natural beauty:

National Museums: The Tokyo National Museum, Kyoto National Museum, and other major museums provide accessibility features such as wheelchair ramps, elevators, and accessible exhibits.

Gardens and Parks: Many famous gardens and parks in Japan, such as Shinjuku Gyoen National Garden and Kenrokuen Garden, have accessible pathways, wheelchair rentals, and designated viewing areas.

Accessible Castles: Some castles, like Himeji Castle and Matsumoto Castle, have made efforts to improve accessibility by installing ramps and elevators. However, it's important to note that historical structures may have limitations due to their architectural design.

Accessible Onsen: Some hot spring resorts offer accessible bathing facilities, including ramps, handrails, and private bathing options. Research and inquire in advance to find suitable options.

Communication and Language:

Navigating a foreign country can be easier when equipped with basic language skills and communication strategies:

Language Translation Apps: Utilize translation apps like Google Translate or Microsoft Translator, which can translate text and spoken language to facilitate communication.

Simple Phrases: Learn some basic Japanese phrases related to accessibility, such as "I use a wheelchair" or "Is this accessible?"

Japanese Disability Symbol: Familiarize yourself with the Japanese Disability Symbol, a blue-and-white icon indicating accessibility. This symbol is often displayed on accessible facilities.

Local Etiquette and Respect:

While Japan is generally respectful and accommodating, understanding local customs can enhance your travel experience:

Priority Seating: In public transportation, priority seating is available for individuals with disabilities, pregnant women, and the elderly. Be mindful of these designated seats and offer them to those who need them.

Respect Personal Space: In crowded areas, be considerate of others and respect personal space. Avoid blocking pathways or hindering the movement of other travelers.

Assistance and Politeness: If you require assistance, don't hesitate to ask politely. Japanese people are generally helpful and will do their best to assist you.

Service Animals: Japan recognizes guide dogs for the visually impaired and hearing assistance dogs. Familiarize yourself with the regulations and guidelines regarding their entry and access to public spaces.

Traveling with disabilities in Japan may present certain challenges, but with proper planning and awareness, you can enjoy the beauty and hospitality this country has to offer. Embrace the rich cultural experiences, breathtaking landscapes, and warm encounters that await you in Japan. Remember, accessibility is continually improving, and your visit can contribute to promoting a more inclusive society.

Unique Experiences: Tea Ceremonies, Samurai Lessons, and More

Japan is a country renowned for its rich cultural heritage and traditions. While exploring this fascinating country, there are unique experiences you can partake in that offer a glimpse into Japan's ancient customs and allow you to immerse yourself in its history. This chapter highlights some of the most captivating and memorable experiences you can have during your journey through Japan.

Tea Ceremonies:

Tea ceremonies, also known as Chanoyu or Sado, are highly regarded in Japanese culture. These ceremonies focus on the preparation and presentation of matcha, a powdered green tea. Participating in a tea ceremony provides a serene and contemplative experience. Here's what you can expect:

Ritualistic Preparation: Witness the meticulous process of preparing matcha, including the whisking of the tea powder and the precise pouring of hot water.

Harmonious Atmosphere: Tea ceremonies are often held in serene tea houses or traditional gardens, creating an ambiance of tranquility and harmony.

Cultural Significance: Learn about the history, philosophy, and etiquette associated with tea ceremonies. Tea masters often explain the symbolism and cultural significance behind each step of the ceremony.

Participatory Experience: Depending on the type of tea ceremony, you may have the opportunity to try whisking the tea yourself or engaging in traditional Japanese sweets (wagashi) alongside the tea.

Samurai Lessons:

For those fascinated by Japan's feudal era and warrior traditions, participating in a samurai lesson offers a unique glimpse into the life and skills of these legendary warriors. Here's what you can expect from a samurai experience:

Historical Insights: Learn about the samurai's code of conduct (bushido), their weaponry, and the principles that guided their lives.

Martial Arts Training: Engage in a hands-on samurai training session, where you can learn basic sword techniques, archery, or other martial arts associated with the samurai.

Dress in Traditional Attire: Some samurai experiences provide the opportunity to dress in traditional samurai armor or don a kimono, allowing you to truly immerse yourself in the role.

Cultural Appreciation: Gain a deeper understanding of Japanese history, traditions, and the values upheld by the samurai through the guidance of knowledgeable instructors.

Zen Meditation:

Zen meditation, known as Zazen, is a practice rooted in Buddhist philosophy that focuses on mindfulness and self-reflection. Engaging in Zen meditation allows you to experience a moment of stillness and inner peace. Here's what you can expect:

Instruction and Guidance: Learn the proper posture, breathing techniques, and concentration methods from experienced Zen practitioners.

Temple Visits: Many Zen meditation experiences take place in serene Zen temples, providing a tranquil setting conducive to meditation.

Insight into Buddhism: Discover the principles of Buddhism and the philosophies that guide Zen practice, such as impermanence and mindfulness.

Self-Discovery: Through Zen meditation, you can cultivate a sense of self-awareness, mental clarity, and emotional balance.

Traditional Crafts Workshops:

Japan is renowned for its traditional crafts, and participating in a workshop offers a hands-on experience where you can learn from skilled artisans. Here are some popular traditional crafts workshops you can consider:

Pottery: Try your hand at crafting pottery using traditional techniques such as wheel throwing or hand-building. You can create your unique ceramic piece to take home as a memento.

Calligraphy: Learn the art of Japanese calligraphy, known as Shodo. Explore the brush strokes and techniques used to write Kanji characters or express a specific phrase or poem.

Kimono Dressing: Experience the elegance of

wearing a traditional kimono and learn the intricate process of dressing in this iconic Japanese garment.

Washi Papermaking: Discover the art of traditional Japanese papermaking, known as Washi. Learn how to create beautiful sheets of paper using natural fibers and techniques passed down through generations.

Cultural Festivals:

Japanese festivals, or Matsuri, are vibrant and lively celebrations held throughout the year. These festivals showcase the country's rich cultural heritage and offer a unique opportunity to engage with local traditions. Here's what you can expect from attending a cultural festival:

Traditional Performances: Witness dynamic performances such as taiko drumming, traditional dances (Bon Odori), or theatrical displays like Kabuki or Noh.

Street Food and Stalls: Indulge in a variety of delectable street food offerings, from savory treats like takoyaki (octopus balls) to sweet delights like taiyaki (fish-shaped pastries).

Processions and Parades: Experience the excitement of parades featuring beautifully decorated floats, portable shrines, and participants dressed in vibrant traditional costumes.

Fireworks Displays: Many festivals culminate in mesmerizing fireworks displays, offering a spectacle of colors and lights against the night sky.

These unique experiences provide an

opportunity to delve deeper into Japan's culture, history, and traditional practices. Whether you choose to participate in a tea ceremony, learn the ways of the samurai, engage in Zen meditation, explore traditional crafts, or join in the festivities of a cultural festival, each experience promises to leave you with cherished memories and a deeper appreciation for Japan's rich heritage.

Saying Farewell: Reflecting on Your Journey and Future Plans

As your journey through Japan comes to an end, it's important to take a moment to reflect on the incredible experiences you've had and the memories you've created. Saying farewell to a country that has captivated your heart can be bittersweet, but it also marks the beginning of new adventures and the opportunity to plan for future travels. This chapter offers guidance on how to bid farewell to Japan while cherishing your journey and looking forward to what lies ahead.

Embrace Reflection:

Take some time to reflect on your journey through Japan. Consider the places you've visited, the people you've met, and the moments that left a lasting impression on you. Reflect on the cultural insights you've gained, the personal growth you've experienced, and the lessons learned during your time in Japan. Embrace the memories and the impact this journey has had on you.

Capture Memories:

Ensure you have captured your journey through Japan in various forms. Review your photographs, videos, and written reflections to relive the moments and emotions you experienced. Organize and preserve these memories in a way that allows you to revisit them in the future. Consider creating a travel journal or a digital album to hold the stories and visuals of your adventure.

Express Gratitude:

Show gratitude to the people who made your journey through Japan special. Thank the locals who extended their kindness and assistance, the guides and experts who shared their knowledge, and the individuals who helped you navigate through unfamiliar territories. Consider leaving positive reviews or sending personal notes of appreciation to express your gratitude for the remarkable experiences you've had.

Share Your Stories:

Share your experiences and insights with others. Talk to friends, family, and fellow travelers about the highlights of your journey, the hidden gems you discovered, and the lessons you learned. Consider creating a blog, writing articles, or using social media platforms to share your travel stories with a wider audience. By sharing your experiences, you can inspire others to embark on their own journeys to Japan.

Incorporate Japanese Influences:

Bring a piece of Japan back with you as a tangible reminder of your journey. Whether it's a traditional souvenir, a piece of artwork, or a Japanese-inspired item for your home, these tangible mementos can serve as symbols of the transformative experience you had in Japan. Incorporating elements of Japanese culture into your daily life can help you keep the spirit of your journey alive.

Plan for Future Travels:

While bidding farewell to Japan, start planning

your next adventure. Reflect on the aspects of travel that ignited your passion and consider the destinations that resonate with you. Research other countries or regions that offer similar cultural richness, natural beauty, or historical significance. Begin outlining your future travel plans and set goals to continue exploring the world.

Stay Connected:

Maintain connections with the people you've met during your time in Japan. Whether it's through social media, email exchanges, or even planning future meet-ups, staying connected with the individuals who shared moments of your journey can foster lifelong friendships and provide opportunities for future collaborations or reunions.

Remember that bidding farewell to Japan is not the end but rather a continuation of your travel experiences. The lessons learned, memories made, and personal growth achieved will forever be a part of you. Cherish the time you spent in Japan and carry the spirit of its culture, traditions, and hospitality with you as you embark on future adventures. As you close this chapter, keep your heart open to the wonders that await you in the world beyond Japan's borders.

Printed by Libri Plureos GmbH in Hamburg,
Germany